# Pearson–Marr Archetype Indicator® Instrument and Scoring Sheet

## Instructions for completing the PMAI® Instrument

The PMAI® instrument is designed to help people better understand themselves and others by identifying the different, and sometimes contradictory, themes that shape their lives. Each theme is named for its central character (or archetype) and that character's way of interpreting events and acting in the world. The twelve archetypes included in the PMAI instrument are equally valuable and each brings with it a special gift. No one is better or worse than another. Therefore, there are no right or wrong answers or better or worse answers. As you respond to the statements in the instrument, keep the following in mind:

- Work as quickly as is comfortable; your first reaction is often the best response.

- Please do not skip any items as they may invalidate your results.

- If you are unsure of an item, make your best determination based on your understanding of the statement and then continue.

- Answer what is true for you in the last few months, not your whole life or just today.

- Be careful to answer questions as you are, rather than how you would like to be or as someone else would like you to be.

PMAI®

## Totals from Instrument

1 _____ (Innocent)

2 _____ (Orphan)

3 _____ (Warrior)

4 _____ (Caregiver)

5 _____ (Seeker)

6 _____ (Lover)

7 _____ (Destroyer)

8 _____ (Creator)

9 _____ (Ruler)

10 _____ (Magician)

11 _____ (Sage)

12 _____ (Jester)

**1** *If you have not done so, please total the separate columns (1–12) in the instrument booklet. Transfer your totals to the appropriate blanks.*

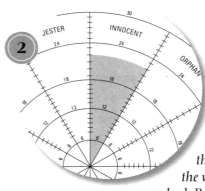

**2**

*You now have a number value assigned to each archetype in the list. For each archetype, shade in the appropriate area in the wheel that corresponds with the number value from the list. For example, if the value next to Innocent is 22, then shade in the Innocent section of the wheel from 22 to the center of the wheel. Repeat for all twelve archetypes.*

**3** *For validation and interpretation of your results, please consult chapter 3 of this booklet.*

# What Story Are You Living?

# What Story Are You Living?

A Guide to Interpreting Results from the
Pearson–Marr Archetype Indicator® Assessment

CAROL S. PEARSON & HUGH K. MARR

CENTER FOR APPLICATIONS OF PSYCHOLOGICAL TYPE, Inc.
2815 NW 13th St., Suite 401 · Gainesville, FL 32609 · 1.800.777.2278 · www.capt.org

© 2007 Carol S. Pearson and Hugh K. Marr
© 2003 Archetype Icons. Center for Applications of Psychological Type, Inc.
Second Printing 2009

Published by
Center for Applications of Psychological Type, Inc.
2815 NW 13th Street, Suite 401
Gainesville FL 32609
352.375.0160
www.capt.org

Printed in the United States.

Center for Applications of Psychological Type, Inc. and CAPT are trademarks or registered trademarks of the Center for Applications of Psychological Type in the United States and other countries.

Pearson-Marr Archetype Indicator and PMAI are registered trademarks of Carol S. Pearson and Hugh K. Marr in the United States and other countries.

Myers-Briggs Type Indicator, Myers-Briggs, and MBTI are trademarks or registered trademarks of the MBTI Trust, Inc. in the United States and other countries.

Library of Congress Cataloging-in-Publication Data

Pearson, Carol, 1944–
   What story are you living? : a workbook and guide to interpreting results from the Pearson-Marr Archetype Indicator instrument / Carol S. Pearson, Hugh K. Marr.
        p. cm.
Includes bibliographical references and index.
ISBN-13: 978-0-935652-78-9
ISBN-10: 0-935652-78-7
1. Pearson-Marr Archetype Indicator. 2. Archetype (Psychology)  I. Marr, Hugh K., 1949- II. Title.

BF698.8.P37P44 2006
   155.2'64--dc22

                                                                                          2006022658

# Table of Contents

**CHAPTER 8**

# The Twelve Archetypes / 81

**CHAPTER 9**

# Resources for Expanding Your Skills / 155

# Preface

∘   ∘   ∘

*What Story Are You Living?* is based on a model for understanding the stories we live that was originally developed by Carol Pearson and described in *The Hero Within* and augmented in *Awakening the Heroes Within.* Inspired by the contribution of the Myers-Briggs Type Indicator® instrument to helping people understand themselves and others, Carol decided to develop an instrument that could help people recognize the archetypal stories that are present in their lives. That's when psychologist Hugh Marr joined the project, focusing his doctoral dissertation around the development of the Pearson-Marr Archetype Indicator® (PMAI®) assessment.

Together and separately, we have used the PMAI® assessment with individuals in all walks of life and for a variety of purposes. We have worked with leaders, couples, friends, families, work teams, and other groups. We have found that when people share their stories, they are able to better understand one another and work cooperatively in relationships and at tasks. They become clearer about their callings and the central purposes to their lives, and they are better able to meet whatever challenges come their way.

Although *What Story Are You Living?* was originally intended to be a brief guide to understanding PMAI® scores based on our earlier work, this version has become much more than just a guide. It reflects new knowledge and perspectives that have come from the experience of working with the PMAI® instrument over many years.

Although interpretations of PMAI® results can be complex, this workbook provides the basic information you need to begin your understanding of how to use archetypes in your life. As you read about archetypes in this guide, you will understand how different archetypes are active in various ways throughout your life. Your expression of archetypes may vary depending upon your situation and your stage of life. By taking the PMAI® assessment every six months to a year and tracking the changes in the stories you are living, you can keep current with your own growth and development.

When friends, co-workers, or family members also take the PMAI® instrument, you can share your stories, which will lead to better understanding and communication. Many people find that discussing their results with others is both fun and meaningful, allowing people to feel closer and to work together more effectively. It is a nonthreatening way to share with others what matters to you and what you value most deeply. In the same manner, you come to learn about the inner lives of those close to you, thus expanding your horizons and seeing things from their perspectives.

The instrument is written at an eighth-grade reading level, which means that it can be used with adolescents as well as with adults. Therapists and coaches can use it with clients, teachers and counselors with students, and group facilitators with teams and other small groups. Some people use the instrument in workshops or even at social gatherings to encourage people to begin sharing at a deeper level.

Whether you use the PMAI® assessment in an introductory way or go deeper, we hope that working through the guidebook greatly enhances your life. The primary purpose of this work is to help people live consciously, rather than simply live out unconscious patterns that may keep them from fulfilling their full potential. A secondary purpose is to promote the kind of awareness that allows individuals, groups, and societies to gain the narrative intelligence to ask themselves: is this the story I (we) want to live? And, if the answer is yes, we encourage you to live that story in one of its positive forms. If no, we hope you will be able to shift the story to something that promotes a better life for yourself and all those whose lives you touch. **O**

*Carol S. Pearson and Hugh K. Marr*

# CHAPTER 1

# How and Why We Live Stories

o   o   o

*We are storytelling creatures. Listen to people talking in a restaurant, at the water cooler, or at a party, and you will quickly find that the majority of what they say is in the form of stories. We connect by telling each other stories. We can better understand ourselves by recognizing and exploring our life narratives. Your life story is the tale that you repeatedly tell yourself about who you are, what you want, what you can and cannot do. Before the second year of life, we are sensitive to the tone of stories lived around us, and we have already begun collecting thousands of images that resonate emotionally with us in some important way. At first the plots are inconsistent and illogical—much as our dreams continue to be. By elementary school, we follow particular rules about the beginning, middle, and ending* of stories; so they begin to make sense. By adolescence, we tell ourselves consistent stories about our lives that define who we are, how we came to be that way, and where we are headed. We see events that we can recount as vignettes of our central life narrative.

Although there are as many variations of life stories as there are individuals, people tend to create narratives according to a finite number of templates. Christopher Booker, for example, in his compendium *The Seven Basic Plots*, makes a compelling case based on world literature for seven types of stories (e.g., the quest, overcoming the monster, comedy, etc.). Others have identified fifteen or even thirty-two narrative types. The point is that while we may argue whether some story types are really variants on other types, there are a very small number of general narrative forms in the world's literature. The same is true of characters and the roles they play. How can this be?

In the 1960s there was a television series called *Naked City* (1958–1963). It was a series of dramas, all of which took place in New York City. Each week the show ended with the tag line "There are eight million stories in the Naked City. This has been one of them." Contrary to what may have been the producer's hope, the show did not last for anything close to eight million episodes. But even though there are far more than eight million stories in New York City–or in any city–they are all variations on relatively few characters and themes. It is as if there are only a few story templates that have been passed down to us over the millennia during which we have inhabited earth.

In the first part of the twentieth century, the psychiatrist Carl Jung recognized the universality of characters and situations. Just as there are certain musical tones that sound resonant across cultures, there are similarly a universal set of roles, situations, and themes that are recognizable by everyone. These universal templates are called "archetypes," which are derived from the Greek archetypos, meaning "the original pattern or model of which all things of the same type are representations or copies" (*Merriam-Webster Collegiate Dictionary, 11th Edition*). Jung,

**READ ME!**

**If you would like more detailed information and background
about using the Pearson–Marr Archetype Indicator® Instrument,
including reliability and validity studies, please refer to the
PMAI® Manual (see resources in chapter 9).**

o  o  o

and many after him, saw that these stories which recur in literature and art are the same narratives we as humans live. For example, we all recognize the love story whether we encounter it in a movie, an opera, or a novel. And when we fall in love, we experience for ourselves what that story is about. When we are in a loving relationship, we not only learn major life lessons (in this case about intimacy, sensuality, pleasure, and commitment), but we also feel a sense of connection to all the other people who have ever loved deeply. While each love is different, there is a deep pattern that transcends these differences. When we understand the stories and recognize their universality, we can connect with each other at deeper and more conscious levels, using the archetypal stories as the foundation.

This may be especially true of the sacred myths of cultures, which are particularly archetypal, as they express in metaphor people's actual experiences. These stories do not necessarily have to be taken literally. Rather, the concrete outward actions symbolize inner experiences. We read the story of an outward journey and something resonates in our inward journey.

This is why people talk about "life journeys," even if they have never outwardly left the town where they grew up. People connect immediately to a journey story from another culture, finding resonance with the characters and the form and the phases of the journey, even if the particular details are not familiar. Such stories influence people for good or ill. Archetypal stories can provide breakthroughs in insight and move people toward harmony and success, but such stories are equally able to tempt people toward less productive, even destructive, behaviors. Either way, an understanding of the archetypal narrative can enhance insight or enable people to break free of destructive patterns.

The archetypal stories described in this guidebook as assessed by the PMAI® assessment are those associated with the hero's journey, which is a model for the individuation process (the process of finding yourself and connecting to your depth and your full potential). They are named by the primary character in each story: Innocent, Orphan, Warrior, Caregiver, Seeker, Lover, Destroyer, Creator, Ruler, Magician, Sage, and Jester.

⊙　⊙　⊙

## Example of a Mythic (Archetypal) Story

We will use the retelling of a Native American story to illustrate the idea of archetypal narratives and characters. This story, which will help you better understand and apply the concepts of the archetypal stories, is interrupted with explanations of how to identify and understand an archetypal story.

## THE STORY OF LITTLE MOUSE

*Once there was a Little Mouse. Little Mouse lived on the great wide grassy prairie with
many other mice, each scurrying hither and yon, gathering seeds and dropping seeds.*

So begins the Plains Indian story of *Little Mouse* (alternately known as *Jumping Mouse*)–a
tale that has been retold by various people, including John Steptoe in *The Story of Jumping Mouse*
and by Hyemeyohsts Storm in the beautifully illustrated book *Seven Arrows*. As the story begins,
we are given a picture of the great expanse of the plains and its contrast with the fruitless and
petty bustling of everyday life.

The stories of our lives, like stories and dramas everywhere, have scenes and settings–
both physical and ideological. When you hear a tale that begins "long ago and far away" you
are prepared for certain things, such as the suspension of the familiar and a beckoning into the
universality of what is to come. In the same way, when you hear the first lines of a story about
a woman growing up on a small Amish farm in Pennsylvania, you are prepared to hear the
influence of a more specific and realistic setting.

*Little Mouse and his friends went about their activities, all the while darting into holes
whenever wind, in waving the tall grasses, cast rippling shadows on the land. Each moving shadow led to even more frantic scurrying for dread that this shadow was the shadow
of the eagles circling high above.*

All stories have a tone, an emotional atmosphere. In the beginning of *Little Mouse*, the
underlying tone is tinged with fear, which is unsuccessfully warded off by frantic, helpless
busy work. The environments in our lives also have emotional climates: think for a minute
of the predominant climate at your place of work, or at school. Is it frantic and helpless, like
Little Mouse's prairie; is it connected and supportive; or is it isolative and competitive? Families
also have an atmosphere. The emotional chords of all situations–growing up, daily life, work
environment–provide narrative tone to the story of your life.

*Beneath the swishing sound of wind in the long grass, beneath the scampering and chat-
tering of the mice, Little Mouse noticed another, constant sound–a steady roar. The other
mice said, "It is nothing. Go back to gathering your seeds." Or, "What sound? There's no
roar." Sometimes they whispered among themselves, "There must be something wrong
with Little Mouse–all this talk of a roar."*

*But try as he might, Little Mouse could not ignore the quiet roar.*

Some stories focus primarily on one archetypal story (for example, the Warrior overcoming an adversary). Others, like this one, show a character sequentially living out plot structures, and in so doing, expanding and growing. At this story's beginning, the mice were living

an Innocent story, oblivious to the larger world. Anything that interfered with their world view had to be rejected or denied for fear of what changes might be encouraged by recognizing it.

When Little Mouse begins to ask about the "roar," a problem and a conflict is introduced. All stories are about problems and how they are negotiated.

> *Little Mouse decided that despite what his fellows said, he had to find the source of the roaring. And so it was with great apprehension he left the rocks and the seeds and the hiding places of the mice and set out across the wide grassland, following the roar in his ears.*

Sometimes what is seen as a personal problem also becomes a calling–a calling to begin one's life journey in a new and unexplored direction. This calling is an event that initiates the journey.

> *Little Mouse traveled for hours and miles across the wide prairie, darting from grass clump to rock, ever fearful lest he see the shadow of an eagle. Guided only by the roaring in his ears, he darted and zigzagged toward where the sound grew louder and louder. Finally he reached a place where the roaring was so loud that he could not even hear his heart thumping from exertion and from the fear of the eagle. He stopped and sniffed, unsure what to do. It was then that above the din he heard a voice, and it was calling his name!*

> *"Little Mouse," said the voice, "crouch down as low as you can and jump up as high as you can." Not knowing what else to do, Little Mouse obeyed. He crouched down as low as he possibly could, and then leaped as high as he could.*

> *In an instant that lasted a lifetime so great was its effect, Little Mouse's head peeked over the top of the grass. He saw a rushing, boiling torrent of water stretching almost to the horizon. And in a quiet pool in the midst of the tumult floated a lily pad. Crouching on the lily pad was the owner of the mysterious voice–Frog. And behind the lily pad, behind the torrent, glowing in royal purple stood a sight that, even more than the magnificent river, made Little Mouse suck in his breath. It was a glimpse of the sacred mountains. Little Mouse fell into the cold water at the edge of the stream. "Little Brother," called the Frog.*

> *"Now you have a new name–now your name is 'Jumping Mouse'!"*

Having heeded the calling, one's perceptions are changed; life is no longer the same. In effect, one has entered a new phase in one's story. Like Adam and Eve awakening to the knowledge of good and evil, there is no going back in full to the archetypal story of the Innocent.

The frog, as one of the helpers along Little Mouse's journey, marks Little Mouse's new world view by giving him a new name, Jumping Mouse. Changing the world by an alteration in perception and in language is the hallmark of the power of the archetype called the Magician.

> *Little Mouse scurried back toward the land of the mice. He ran as quickly as he could, no longer mindful of the eagles. He had to tell all the other mice of the great world he had seen.*

> *But upon his return he was surprised to find the other mice seemed to fear him. They whispered that he was crazy. And worse, that he was wet and bedraggled because he had no doubt been caught by some predator and spit out. And if he was not even good enough for a predator, of what use was he to them?*

Jumping Mouse is now different from his fellows, and this scares them enough that they ostracize him. Jumping Mouse has become an Orphan. Often the story of the Orphan is ushered in by a calling to a larger story, which results in betrayal and fear on the part of one's former community or tribe.

> *In time Jumping Mouse's fur dried. But his fellow mice still avoided him; and try as he might, Jumping Mouse could not ignore the roaring of the great river, nor could he forget the sacred mountains.*

> *He decided that no matter the risk he had to make his way to the sacred mountains. And so he gathered a few seeds and set out across the wide prairie.*

The story of the Seeker is the tale of the quest. Whether it is *Treasure Island* or *Star Wars*, the Seeker feels compelled to undergo the journey, which almost always begins in wild and foreign territory.

> *Jumping Mouse moved across the uncharted grassland, scurrying from the shelter of rocks to bushes and back again. All the while Jumping Mouse kept one nervous eye on the ground, watching for the fast moving shadow of Eagle.*

> *After he had traveled in this manner for many hours, he began to hear a loud, regular snorting and whistling. At first he crouched in fear; then, seeing no danger, he carefully crept from behind a rock and peered over a small rise.*

> *There he saw a large hill of fur; and as he slowly approached, he noticed that it began to rise and fall gently. It was then that he realized that what he had taken for a hill was in fact the most awesome beast he had ever seen. The beast did not seem to notice Jumping Mouse; indeed, as Jumping Mouse approached, he saw that the huge eyes were closed.*

> *Ever so carefully Jumping Mouse crept to the base of one of the huge ears. "Hello!" he shouted.*

*With a deafening snort, the beast shook its head and Jumping Mouse tumbled over and over in the grass. "Why, hello, Little Brother!" thundered the huge beast. "I am Buffalo, and I used to rule all the prairie from horizon to horizon. But a great sickness has befallen me, and I am confined to this small valley, for every time I try to rise. . ." With these words Buffalo opened his huge jaws wide, and Jumping Mouse saw molars as big as his head. The beast was about to eat him! Jumping Mouse turned and ran as fast as he could. When he dared to look back, he saw that not only was buffalo's mouth now closed, his eyes were as well. Once again the hill of fur rose and fell to the snorting and whistling.*

*Jumping Mouse crept back and again shouted into the huge ear. "Hello, Brother Buffalo!" This time Buffalo opened his eyes without knocking Jumping Mouse off.*

*"Oh," he said, "I am so sorry. It's this sickness. I can hardly hold my eyes open. I have been told that the only thing which can cure me is the eye of a mouse. But I don't even know what a mouse is, let alone where to find one between naps. Could you help me?" And with this plaintive request, the buffalo was once again fast asleep.*

*Jumping Mouse thought, "He is so big, and so wonderful; but his life has been stolen by the terrible sickness. And I am but a Little Mouse; and besides, I have two eyes. Surely I could spare one for such a noble beast as Buffalo." And no sooner had Jumping Mouse made up his mind but one of his eyes popped painlessly out of its socket; and Brother Buffalo shook his head and began slowly to rise.*

Here we have the story of the Caregiver, willing to sacrifice even his own body for the health and succor of another. Often in the story of the Caregiver, the self is never valued as highly as others. Perhaps we do not literally give away an eye, but most of us probably have made some sacrifice for another in the process of learning to be altruistic.

*"Little Brother," said the buffalo, "where are you going?"*

*"I am traveling to the Sacred Mountains," replied Jumping Mouse.*

*"The prairie is my home; I cannot go up into the hills. But I would be honored to escort you to the edge of the great prairie. Just run along the ground under me; you can move in a straight line, and have no fear for the Eagle."*

*And so Jumping Mouse ran under the huge buffalo. The thundering hooves tore great clods of tough prairie sod, throwing them in all directions. Jumping Mouse lived in dread, sure that at any moment one of the great hooves would surely trample him into the earth.*

*At the edge of the great prairie they stopped. "You need never have feared," said Buffalo, noticing how his companion trembled. "I know at all moments exactly where each hoof will land. And now I must take your leave. Thank you, Little Brother, for restoring my life."*

*Jumping Mouse crouched in the shadow of a small tree. The hills undulated almost to the horizon; but there, just on the horizon line, Jumping Mouse saw the royal purple of the sacred mountains.*

*It was then that he heard a loud chuckling. He peered from behind the tree to see a huge furry beast. This creature was not so large as Buffalo, but what he lacked in size he made up for in the ferocity of a long narrow snout glistening with sharp teeth. The creature saw Jumping Mouse at the same time; there was no chance to escape, so Jumping Mouse boldly stepped forward.*

*"Hello, Brother," said Jumping Mouse.*

*"Why, hello!" said the beast. "my name is . . . Is . . . Wait a moment, don't tell me. . . ."*

*"I can't tell you; but I can tell you my name is Jumping Mouse."*

*"Pleased to meet you. Did you say mouse? I have been told that the eye of a mouse is the only thing that can help me with something, I forget what."*

*"Memory?" suggested Jumping Mouse.*

*"Yes, Coyote!"*

*"Coyote?" puzzled Little Mouse.*

*"Yes, that's my name. And what did you say your name was?"*

*Jumping Mouse was quiet. Here was another magnificent creature—magical but wounded. But if he were to lose his other eye. . . . Jumping Mouse decided in a moment.*

*"Brother Coyote," determined Jumping Mouse, "I am a mouse, and you may have my eye to heal your memory. And with that Jumping Mouse's other eye sprung from its place.*

It is common to stories of the quest that the hero meets helpers along the way. But here the helpers have all been wounded (Orphaned) in some significant way that prevents them from functioning well in their daily lives. It is the giving of himself as Caregiver that restores the other creatures. The irony is that Jumping Mouse, as Caregiver, donates the very thing which he most values—for it is the sight of the sacred mountains that he pursues. In return for his gift, he cannot yet know that he will receive a gift of help that will ultimately be worth more than the sight he relinquishes.

*"Thank you, Jumping Mouse," said Coyote. "I am afraid that all I have to give you in return is safe passage through the hills to the foot of the sacred mountains. I do not live in the mountains, so I can only take you to their feet."*

*And so Jumping Mouse clung to Coyote's long tail while he trotted through the hills into the base of the sacred mountains.*

*"I will leave you here, behind this rock, where you will be safe for a time from the eagles."*

*"Thank you, Brother," said Jumping Mouse. He sat for a long time and listened to the wind and felt the bliss from being at last among the Sacred Mountains. Finally he ventured from behind the rock.*

*Although he could no longer see it, he felt the shadow almost immediately, followed by a rush of wind. He was not sure what he had expected; surely great pain and terror as the claws of the eagle stove him to the ground.*

*He lay for a long time before opening his eyes. To his surprise, although everything was very blurry, he could see! It was then that he heard a familiar voice.*

*"Little Brother! Bend down as low as you can and jump as high as you can!"*

*He obeyed, crouching low and jumping as high as he could. To his surprise, he did not fall back, but instead got caught by the wind and carried higher and higher. He looked down on the rocks, then the mountain. From that height the details were sharp and clear, even though he was now high above them.*

*Behind the rocks a mountain stream twisted and gurgled. And there, on a lily pad in a quiet pool, sat his old friend the frog.*

*"Little Brother!" called Frog. "now you have a new name! Now your name is Eagle!"*

(Adapted from *Jumping Mouse* by John Steptoe)

The story of *Little Mouse* is both a story of quest and a story of transformation. There are many small shifts leading to the final transformation. In many cultures the major transformations of self are marked by a change of name, just as Little Mouse became Jumping Mouse, and, finally, Eagle. The new name tells us something important about the sight he lost and what kind of sight he regained. The eyes of mice are designed to see close up, as they are built close to the ground and must see down into the grasses for food. The eyes of eagles are designed for distant sight as they soar high in the air. When Little Mouse loses his near-sighted eyes, he feels only the loss of what he has known. Only later does he, and we, understand that his loss is preparation for a different quality of sight. The new name allows both Little Mouse and those around him to recognize this achievement.

We have vestiges of such deep naming today in the way people assume a new title upon the completion of a certain course of study (such as with master's or doctoral degrees); the achievement of rank in the military or police (corporal, sergeant, commander); and the choice of some women to take a new name upon marriage. Notice that this custom of naming to mark a change persists more among the oldest institutions in our society (military, academia, marriage). Even though we no longer change our names in most life transitions, our own life stories must grow and change as we mature.

Also as in the story of *Little Mouse*, the story we tell ourselves has a plot that unfolds in four phases: a preparatory time (living among the other mice); followed by some initiating event, or calling, that starts us on our journey (the roaring sound of the great river); the journey itself which proceeds by attempts to attain a goal; and, finally, the return (Jumping Mouse returns to his fellows after witnessing the Great River; and the return of the Eagle to the prairie is implied in Little Mouse). At any one time, our lives may contain one story or several. It is estimated that over the course of our lives, each one of us will have between five and fifteen life stories, most of which often are variations of the twelve most common archetypal stories. Or, alternatively, a person's life may contain one central story augmented by shorter ones that share a similarity of plot and of character.

The theme of *Little Mouse* is transformation. You will find as you come to understand archetypes that you may have a story that is predominant, but you may also find that there are many subthemes. The major issues underlying the themes often relate to difficult human polarities, such as how we balance connection and control, communion and agency, love and power, realism and optimism, trust and caution, altruism and self-interest and so on. Even beneath these themes are deep needs and desires that motivate us to take journeys in order to find what we desire. In this way, archetypal stories provide models of how to move from desire to fulfillment. What makes the plot interesting is the need to do so in ways that respect both sides of a polarity. For example, if you have a need for control and live a Warrior or Ruler story to get it, you may end up forgetting to bond and connect with others. So you may fulfill the desire to your detriment, ending up powerful, but lonely. However, if you can simultaneously *also* live an affiliative Lover story that allows you to have intimate connections, you may achieve both power and relationships.

The characters represent parts of ourselves; they are chosen primarily as aspects of twelve common archetypal characters that we imbue with specific traits and ideals based upon our own lives. Each character brings with it a particular set of plots. It is as if your larger self, which encompasses all that you are or potentially may be, as well as your connection with the universe, acts as casting director to choose those aspects of yourself most relevant to a particular stage of your journey.

○   ○   ○

## Living the Stories in Everyday Life:
## Stages and Situations

When we are living a particular story, we tend to see the world from its vantage point. What we notice in the world and what actions we think make sense grow naturally from that story. For example, if a student who is living a Warrior story is having a difficult time with another student, she may react in a strong and challenging way, defending her own position. If this student were living a Caregiver story, however, she might instead show concern for what was causing the other person to be difficult, seeking to understand and reassure. When we develop narrative intelligence, we are able to see why we react the way we do and understand the different assumptions and behaviors of others.

There are a host of characters and situations from which these stories are drawn. Such characters have come to be known as *archetypes*, and they define basic stories, although for each person the details will be unique. These archetypes can be looked at as guides that help us know when we are on our best path and taking the most appropriate action. Your PMAI® results help you identify these characters as a way to make sense out of the stories you are living, which allows you to create a richer and more satisfying life.

Many people recognize over time that there is one story that provides the central meaning and purpose of their lives. In addition, other stories are lived out at different times and places. If you think about it, you may notice that different stages of life have offered you new situations, new scenery, new people to be with, even the unfolding of a new storyline. You can see such situations as a stage set, with costumes and supporting characters that seem to pull you into a story line (the plot to be lived out). Such settings have immense power. For example, you may find that when you go back to visit your parents, particularly if they still live in the house where you grew up and have kept familiar things, that you regress and start acting as you did as a child while you are visiting them. Similarly, when you get a new job in a new place, you may find yourself acting (and maybe even dressing) differently than you did previously and learning new behaviors, skills, and attitudes.

Certain life stages typically place us in situations that invite us into specific narratives. For example, if you had a very happy childhood, you likely lived the story of the Innocent. Others were caring for you, and you simply had to trust their wisdom, experiment, and learn what to do to succeed. Living this story provided you with a baseline sense of trust and optimism about life. If, on the other hand, your childhood was difficult, you may have lived an Orphan story. This does not mean that you were literally orphaned (although it could). Rather it means that the adults in your life were too distracted, unskilled, or wounded to care for you properly (physically, emotionally, or intellectually). In this case, you may have experienced a story that had as its theme the challenge of coping in a situation of minor or major deprivation or wounding. Likely this would provide a baseline approach to life that was more cautious and realistic, even pessimistic. Or, you might have lived both stories–either sequentially (if your life situation changed) or at the same time (if your experience with the caregivers in your life was mixed).

As you grew older, you may have become less dependent upon your parents and other authority figures, wanting to explore your own identity and the world outside. You might even have become somewhat oppositional, especially in your adolescent years. You might think of this as living a Seeker story, which exemplifies the gifts of independence and identity. At roughly this same time in life, you may have become interested in romance; and so you began living out a Lover's story, developing the gifts of intimacy and sensuality. This may have led to marriage and children, in which case you suddenly needed to live the story of the Caregiver, demonstrating the ability to nurture and even sacrifice for others.

The list of stories we may live at different stages of our lives can go on and on. The major point here is that success in life is often determined by how well we live out these stories, for it is in the living that we develop into mature, responsible, moral, and successful adults.

So many people today talk about the need for *character*–in public officials, in the heads of corporations, and in the young. However, character cannot be formed by simply enjoining people to act appropriately. We all know from making New Year's resolutions that simply deciding to do or not to do something is not enough to guarantee success. Becoming good, moral, and successful requires knowledge of how to develop the inner qualities that make it easy to do so. Every life situation carries within it a call to live a story that offers experiences that can make us great–or, conversely, bring out what is petty, small, or harmful within us. It is much easier to avoid the slippery slope of life's negative temptations and traps when we can recognize the positive potential within situations.

The stories identified in this book link everyday life with the great, mythic stories that inform what it means to be human. Many people, however, sleepwalk through stories that emerge naturally in certain life stages and life situations, and consequently they lack a sense of meaning and purpose in their lives. At worst, living in this unconscious way decreases their ability to gain the gifts associated from living the great stories; leaves them feeling alone with their problems; and decreases their ability to become the kind of mature and wise people capable of making a positive difference to their families, friends, community, and field of work. When people lack the ability to know what story they are living, they also may fail to develop the qualities required to take adult responsibility for the state of their families, communities, and the larger world.

When we recognize that we are living a unique personal story, as well as one of the universal great narratives, our lives can be filled with meaning, purpose, and dignity. At the same time, we feel less lonely because we can see that we share commonality with all the people, in all times and places, who have lived through the challenges of that story. Following are two examples of how results from the PMAI asessment can be used to help you understand and possibly change your story.

## Steven's Archetypal Story

Steven has what he considers a very ordinary, not very glamorous job. He sees himself basically as a drudge. His PMAI® results show that he is living a Caregiver story. Reflecting about this, he confides that he has a disabled daughter and a wife who struggles daily with depression. He stays in his job because it enables him to take good care of them, which provides the meaning for his life. In the process, he also shares that he feels gratified by showing kindness to his clientele. When he sees that he is living the same great story (the Caregiver story) that Mother Theresa lived, he stops feeling isolated and discouraged, recognizing he is a person of consequence.

As he understands this, he begins to live the possibilities of this story, wanting to live it thoroughly, rather than grudgingly or half-heartedly. When he does this, he stops acting invisible, which he had done before when he thought himself unimportant. His renewed sense of connection with all the Caregivers (and those they care for) makes him more comfortable with people and confident in his role with them. Soon his caregiving activities are rewarded and his influence is extended. He receives a major promotion and launches a volunteer initiative to address a social problem that has bothered him for some time.

## Joan's Archetypal Story

As in our other example, Joan shares that she too has felt locked into living a Caregiver story, and although she wants to care for her children, she feels there is more to her than that. In her heart, she yearns to live a Creator story. She wants to show more imagination in how she interacts with her family *and* to pursue her love of writing. She has locked herself into the traditional homemaker Caregiver role because that is what she has always been told she should do. Her dissatisfaction is evident in her hunched over posture, the martyred look in her eyes, and the bitter turn of her mouth. Her PMAI® results have helped her recognize how strong the Creator story is in her inner life, and how impoverished she feels because the Creator story has been absent in her outer roles. Little by little, she begins rearranging her life so that she has time to write the magazine articles that are always forming in her head. As she does so—and as they are published—she gradually is transformed. Her posture improves; there is a spring in her step and a smile in her eyes as well as her mouth. She is so much happier that her husband and children feel a new level of lightness and freedom, and their home again feels like a good place to be. In fact, as she lives the story that is right for her, it has ripple effects that help the other people she encounters.

This is the power of the PMAI® assessment when its results are used to help people understand the potential for greatness in the stories they are living, or wish to live. It is our hope that this book will inspire you to identify your greatness and that of others, and in so doing, encourages you to live the life that is most authentically yours.

Before going further, you might find it helpful to know more about archetypes and what we mean when we describe a character or a narrative as archetypal.

o    o    o

## Exploring Archetypal Stories

Archetypes are psychological structures reflected in symbols, images, and themes common to all cultures and all times. You see them in recurring images in art, literature, myths, and dreams. You may experience archetypes directly as different parts of you. If you say that on one hand you want one thing and on the other you want something else, you can give archetypal names to those parts, as they generally communicate desires and motivations common to humans everywhere. Although the potential characters within us are universal, each of us expresses them differently, endowing them with somewhat different styles, traits, and mannerisms. For example, while the Warrior is an archetype, different kinds of Warriors engage in different battles. The Warrior archetype encompasses the Japanese samurai and the American G.I., but it also might include the dedicated biologist racing to find the cure for a life-threatening disease, an advocate for social justice, or the member of a street gang. Each of these Warriors follows a different code of honor, goals, style of dress, and more; nevertheless, all of them are Warriors. The expression of an archetype will be influenced by a person's culture, setting, and time in history, but it will also be a manifestation of his or her individuality.

As aspects of yourself, archetypes can reveal your most important desires and goals. Understanding their expression in your personal myths or stories helps you gain access to unrealized potential, grasp the logic and importance of your life, and increase your empathy for the stories that others live.

In this computer-savvy society, you might think of an archetype as analogous to computer software that helps you to accomplish certain tasks. For example, one program can be used to write a letter, report, or book; other applications help with accounting and reporting. But these programs would be of little help if you confused their functions. Similarly, the Warrior helps people be more focused, disciplined, and tough; the Lover helps them be more passionate, intimate, and loving; while the Jester helps them lighten up and enjoy their lives. When a particular archetype is awakened, you live out its story. In the process, you are able to accomplish definable new tasks. However, it is also important that the archetype be relevant to the task you are facing. If you are going on a date, the evening is not likely to end well if you are combative and act out a war story. Conversely, most people serving as soldiers find it wise not to go into war with the Lover's vulnerability or the Jester's playfulness.

In the ancient world, many people projected the archetypes outwardly onto images of gods and goddesses. In the twentieth century, Jung explored the manifestation of the psychological symbols of archetypes and their role in healing. The Pearson–Marr Archetype Indicator® (PMAI®) assessment makes it easier for you to determine and recognize twelve of the archetypes in your daily life. Understanding these PMAI® archetypes can help you better decode the underlying logic of your life, find greater fulfillment and satisfaction, and free yourself from living out limiting patterns and behaviors. Such knowledge can also increase your insight into other people, thus greatly enhancing your relationships. Most important, understanding these deep psychological structures will make your individuation process (the process of finding yourself and fulfilling your potential) conscious, so that you can gain the gifts associated with maturity, success, and happiness.

When each archetype is active in a person's life, it tends to call forth a particular kind of story or plot. After you have taken the PMAI® instrument, you will want to become familiar with these stories and plots and their archetypal characters by reviewing the archetype descriptions in chapter 8 before proceeding to chapters 2 and 3.

After you have become familiar with the archetypes, you will want to validate and review your results and then develop some practical understanding of how to use this information by doing the exercises in this book. In addition to this introductory book, you may also want to read *Awakening the Heroes Within: Twelve Archetypes to Help Us Find Ourselves and Transform Our World* by Carol S. Pearson, where these archetypes are described in greater detail.

o    o    o
## Archetypal Stages of the Journey

The archetypes and their stories are engaged more subtly as they emerge at different stages of the journey. The mythic hero's journey is outlined in figure 1.1; however, it may or may not

FIGURE 1.1 **The Mythic Hero's Journey**

| | |
|---|---|
| ☐ **Innocent** | Developing the trust, confidence, and optimism to take the journey |
| ☐ **Orphan** | Recognizing that bad things happen and developing realism |
| ☐ **Warrior** | Learning to compete, set goals, and, when necessary, defend yourself |
| ☐ **Caregiver** | Showing care, concern, and, compassion for others; helping |
| ☐ **Seeker** | Being willing to be different; having the courage to try new things |
| ☐ **Lover** | Loving others, being romantic, intimate, and making commitments |
| ☐ **Destroyer** | Letting go and starting over; taking action to end bad situations |
| ☐ **Creator** | Demonstrating imagination, innovation, and cleverness |
| ☐ **Ruler** | Taking charge, being responsible, living according to your values |
| ☐ **Magician** | Changing what happens by altering your own thoughts or behaviors |
| ☐ **Sage** | Thinking clearly, critically, and formulating your own opinions |
| ☐ **Jester** | Enjoying your life and work; being here now |

be the order in which you have lived the stories of these archetypes. The order in which the archetypes are presented is only a typical order in which they may be encountered during the course of development, and thus a logical order in the unfolding of a story. In addition, one or more archetypes may be active throughout your life and become critical to your sense of who you are. To begin your understanding of how archetypes influence your life, review the chart in figure 1.1 and check the archetypes that are most germane to your life at this time.

Note that the hero's journey is a spiral (see figure 1.2), so you may revisit these stages at different times in your life and at different levels of sophistication. Sometimes a particular archetype that you encountered earlier in your life is called for again in a later phase of your life. Therefore, remember that your PMAI® results are not static. They may change in the future. (You might want to retake the instrument every six months or so if you are changing and growing rapidly.)

When you have learned to live a number of stories consciously, you can have access to their gifts and approaches in a flowing way, allowing you to respond well in various situations. Once you have gained reasonable story flexibility, you may notice a variety of archetypes active during any given task or situation. For example, you may begin an endeavor full of hope and optimism (Innocent), but then problems emerge. You face them squarely, noticing who or what is being hurt by whom or by what (Orphan). Then you take action to help those affected (Caregiver) and to remedy or eliminate the cause of the problem (Warrior). If you take the issue deeper, you then pursue cutting-edge solutions (Seeker), make needed

FIGURE 1.2 **The Spiral Journey**

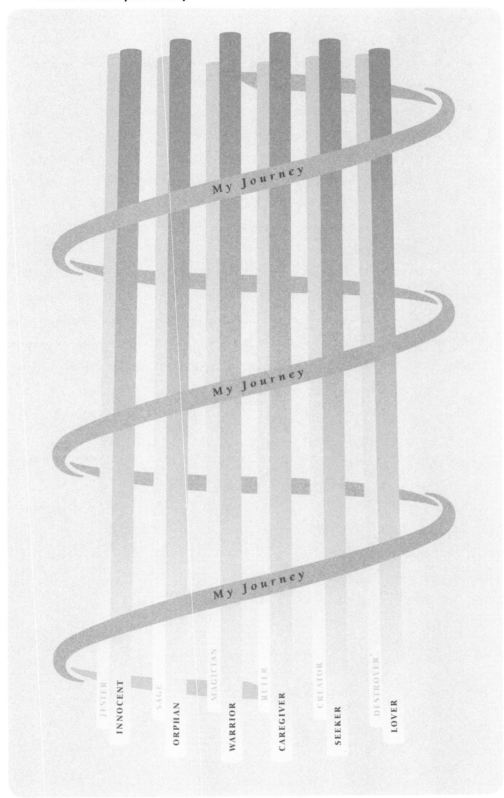

sacrifices (Destroyer), while safe-guarding the people and values you cherish (Lover). You create a new vision (Creator), taking responsibility to implement the plan, using realistic means and timetables (Ruler). To ensure success, you shift your own attitudes and behaviors to be congruent with the outcome you desire (Magician), objectively monitor and evaluate progress (Sage), and make the process as enjoyable as possible, eventually celebrating your success (Jester). While this example demonstrates problem solving using the energies of all the archetypes, only some of the archetypes may be needed in a given situation; as noted previously, you may experience the archetypes in a different order. If a problem is not adequately solved, an additional archetype may need to be available to you and others involved in the situation.

As you review and explore your PMAI® results, you may find it useful to discuss them with a friend or a professional. Psychotherapists, coaches, educators, counselors, and even supervisors and managers can use these theories to assist people in their personal and professional journeys. You can also use the insight derived from understanding archetypes to help guide your children to psychological maturity; to increase communication among family members, friends, or a work team; or to foster environments that encourage people to fulfill their potential. In chapter 4, you will find more information about how to apply working with archetypes in work situations, in relationships, and in your personal life. **O**

### READ ME!

If you have not already done so, you should take the Pearson–Marr Archetype Indicator® (PMAI®) instrument now and record your scores before continuing to read this guide. (You are strongly urged to take the instrument for the first time before reading the archetype descriptions so your answers are fresh and not influenced by what is written here.)

Remove the PMAI® instrument from the front of this book. The PMAI® assessment is also available online at www.capt.org if you are interested in taking it again at a future time to see how your archetypes evolve or if you wish for friends, family members, or co–workers to take the instrument and share results as a group. (For more information on using the PMAI® assessment in groups, please see chapter 5.)

After you complete the instrument, follow the instructions for totaling your score for each archetype. Then transfer your scores for each archetype onto the PMAI® Scoring Worksheet on the back of the question sheet and fill in the pie chart. This will give you a visual picture of the archetypal energies currently active in your life. (You may wish to use crayons or colored pencils or markers to fill in the pie chart.)

Next, refer to the Archetypes Score–Ranges worksheet on the next page. Follow the instructions for listing the archetypes for which you scored highest, lowest, and at midrange. You will want to refer to this summary sheet as you read the archetype descriptions; and then again when you review chapter 3, which provides guidelines for in–depth understanding of your complete PMAI® profile (including scores that are high, low, and at midrange for you).

o  o  o

# Worksheet: Archetype Score–Ranges

| Score | List all Archetypes in this score | Meaning |
|---|---|---|
| 24–30 | Caregiver •<br>ruler → 2<br>sage → 1<br>(Warrior) 2 | For an archetype to have a score in the 24–30 range, all or most of your scores on items related to an archetype would have to be 4s or 5s, thus expressing your strong identification with the archetype. These are the archetypes that are very active in your life, serving as your allies and defining the stories you are living and the gifts you are gaining. One or two may be longstanding in your life and relate to your sense of identity and calling. Others may be related to current life stages or challenges. (If you have no archetypes in the 24–30 category, the top two to four in the 18–23 group are your most active archetypes.) |

| Score | List all Archetypes in this score | Meaning |
|---|---|---|
| 18–23 | ~~warrior~~<br>seeker<br>lover<br>destroyer<br>creator<br>magician<br>jester<br>innocent | For an archetype to have a score in this range, its average score must be in the positive range. Generally, the archetypes in this category are likely to be available to you when you need them but do not determine how you see the world (unless these are your most active archetypes as previously mentioned). These archetypes may also be ascending into consciousness or descending (in which case you may have their virtues). Alternatively, an archetype may be strong, but one-sided in its expression (so that you scored some items high for that archetype and others not so high). |

| Score | List all Archetypes in this score | Meaning |
|---|---|---|
| 12–17 | ~~innocent~~<br>orphan | Scores in this range suggest that these archetypes are not often expressed in your life, and that you consistently disassociate from them in your PMAI® responses. You may have difficulty understanding people who are living out these stories; with circumstances that might call for the strategies or gifts of these archetypes; with ideas, stories, and events that are best understood through the lens of these archetypes. Most of all, these archetypes may simply not be on your screen. |

| Score | List all Archetypes in this score | Meaning |
|---|---|---|
| 6–11 | | Scores below 12 may suggest that you are actively disowning archetypes in this range either because you have internalized a belief they are undesirable or because you have over-expressed them in the past. You may therefore find people distasteful who express these qualities especially the more negative ones. If you act in such ways, you may do so unconsciously. Others may notice these behaviors, but you may not be aware of them yourself. |

# The Archetypal Stories and You

○   ○   ○

*The Pearson-Marr Archetype Indicator® (PMAI®) instrument offers information to help you begin a dialogue with yourself that can lead to greater insight into the complexity and uniqueness of your journey. However, it is not designed to put you into a predetermined box. When you read the descriptors of each archetype in chapter 8, you may reach a conclusion about yourself that differs from your PMAI® score. By reading chapter 2 and by working through some or all of the exercises in chapter 3, you will be able to validate the results from the instrument, which is meant as a guide for exploring how archetypes influence your life. The twelve archetypal categories provide a structure that can increase your self-awareness, but your journey is your own and unlike any other. A good understanding of your PMAI scores is an important first step for increasing your self-awareness.*

Step 2 in chapter 3 ("Validate Your Results") will help you learn ways to resolve any discrepancy between your choice of archetypes and your scores on the PMAI® instrument.

o   o   o
## Discovering the Gifts of Archetypes

The archetypes that are most active in your life are helping you to develop the gifts of that archetype. Some of the most common gifts for each archetype are described in figure 2.1. The simplest, and, for many, the most important usage of the PMAI® assessment is to help you identify your gifts. Archetypal psychologist and Jungian analyst James Hillman in *The Soul's Code* argues that we all have a purpose for being on this earth. One way to discover yours is to notice what you are good at and what energizes and motivates you. Your highest PMAI® scores, then, provide important information about your fundamental way of seeing the world, what you are naturally motivated to do, and, in this way, your fundamental purpose.

If your score for a particular archetype is low, it describes qualities, behaviors, and perspectives that may not be at all like you at this time. To learn more about low scores, see page 45. When a score falls in the midrange, you may relate to some of the traits but recognize that overall the archetype is not what motivates you right now. Sometimes midrange scores reflect archetypes that were more active in the past. Complete descriptions for each of the 12 archetypes begins on page 83.

FIGURE 2.1 **The Archtypal Gifts**

| | |
|---|---|
| **Innocent** | Optimism, trust, hope, faith, simple virtue |
| **Orphan** | Realism, resilience, interdependence, empathy |
| → **Warrior** | Discipline, courage, determination, skill |
| ⤳ **Caregiver** | Community, nurturance, compassion, generosity |
| **Seeker** | Autonomy, ambition, identity, expanded possibilities |
| **Lover** | Passion, commitment, enthusiasm, sensual pleasure |
| **Destroyer** | Metamorphosis, revolution, capacity to let go |
| **Creator** | Creativity, vision, skill, aesthetics, imagination |
| → **Ruler** | Responsibility, sovereignty, control, systems savvy |
| **Magician** | Transformation, catalytic, or healing power |
| ⤳ **Sage** | Wisdom, nonattachment, knowledge, skepticism |
| **Jester** | Humor, life lived in the moment, exuberant joy |

o   o   o

## Understanding Archetypes in Others

As you study your scores and the PMAI® descriptions, you may also recognize ways of thinking and acting that you admire or dislike in others. Such information can help you better understand and relate to those people. If you want to utilize the understanding of mythic stories in this way, you will need to read through all the descriptions to identify those most relevant to the other people you wish to better understand.

Readers often get the most profound "aha's" when they identify the archetypal story or stories being lived out by a nemesis, or by someone with whom they are having difficulty. Recognizing the roles that others play in your story (whether those roles are positive or negative) is helpful for learning to understand people in your life, both personally and professionally.

As you read the descriptions in chapter 8, you can use the answers to the following questions to help you identify the other characters in your archetypal plot. First list the people in the following categories; then note which archetype each primarily represents.

| | People | Archetypes |
|---|---|---|
| *Those you feel extremely drawn to* | | |
| *Those you avoid, dislike, or have conflict with* | | |
| *Your closest family members* | | |
| *Your closest friends* | | |
| *Those you work with most closely* | | |

o   o   o

## Recognizing the Shadow Side of Archetypes

Readers who want to understand themselves at a deeper level may find it interesting to explore the shadow side of archetypal development. The shadow includes the negative side of the archetypes, which can limit perception. And archetypes that are repressed can undermine success by causing us to project disowned characteristics onto others. Following are some pointers on how to avoid pitfalls expressed by the shadow sides of archetypes:

- When an archetype is active in your life, it determines the story that you tend to live. In experiencing that narrative pattern, you gain that archetype's gifts or virtues, and in addition, you learn to face its temptations. The archetype descriptions summarize some of the major forms each archetypal story can take. If you identify what version of the story you are living–and notice its likely ending–you may be able to predict and avoid negative aspects of that archetype and its story. For example, if you are living a Ruler story, you might have a tendency to be controlling (which can be normal for that archetype). If you can see this danger, you can use the strength of the Ruler (the ability to create structures and systems that support people's authentic gifts) to create group harmony and success rather than slip into the Ruler's default desire to dictate what others should do.

- The archetypes you are living determine what you notice around you and the actions you take. Your low scores provide clues to your blind spots–what you might not notice or think to do. If things are not working for you, you may be living out a story that is inappropriate to the situation that you are in. Finding the story that fits the situation may help you break loose and be successful.

- Negative expressions of an archetype may be unskilled attempts to express its more positive side. When you see signs of an archetype's undeveloped and unproductive side in your own or another's behaviors, you can hold in your mind and heart what the positive version of the story looks like and thereby reinforce it.

- Your undeveloped archetypes, especially if they are actively disowned, can be projected onto others who you then see as problems, as scapegoats, as rescuing saviors, or even as evil. When you realize you are projecting, it is best to focus on seeing the good potential within the archetype and then integrate those gifts into your attitudes and behaviors. Sometimes it is helpful to notice the part of you that has some of the negative impulses that you find yourself judging so harshly in others.

- Sometimes archetypes can become so habitual in their expressions that you may succumb to a trancelike state. Under such circumstances, regardless of what happens, you will respond from that archetype's perspective, whether or not it is appropriate or useful to do so. In this case, the archetype is no longer empowering you; instead it has essentially died as an archetype and stayed on as a stereotype, which limits your options. If you notice a story that feels more like an old, unfulfilling habit, rather than something that gives your life meaning and juice, it is best to try to avoid the behaviors associated with that archetype.

- When archetypes are highly active (high scores) or repressed (possible low scores), they can pull you into negative patterns, behaviors, and ways of thinking. Understanding the common traps or pitfalls of archetypes can keep you from falling prey to their temptations. Some of these are summarized in figure 2.2.

FIGURE 2.2 **The Archtypal Pitfalls**

| | |
|---|---|
| **Innocent** | Naiveté, childish dependence, denial, obliviousness |
| **Orphan** | Cynicism, tendency to be victim or victimizer, chronic complaining |
| **Warrior** | Fear of impotence leading to ruthlessness, arrogance |
| **Caregiver** | Martyrdom, enabling others, co-dependence, guilt-tripping |
| **Seeker** | Inability to commit, chronic disappointment, alienation, and loneliness |
| **Lover** | Objectifying others, romance or sex addictions, out of control sexuality |
| **Destroyer** | Doing harm to self or others, out-of-control anger, aggressive tactics |
| **Creator** | Self-indulgence, poverty, perfectionism, prima-donna behaviors |
| **Ruler** | Rigidity, controlling behaviors, an attitude of entitlement, elitism |
| **Magician** | Manipulation, disconnection from reality, cultist guru behaviors |
| **Sage** | Dogmatism, pomposity, impracticality, lack of feeling or empathy |
| **Jester** | Debauchery, irresponsibility, sloth, cruel jokes, con artistry |

o   o   o

## Guidelines for Working with Archetypes

As you explore how archetypes influence your life, keep the following key points in mind.

o Each archetype and each individual has special gifts and challenges. There are no better or worse archetypes.

o PMAI® scores are meant as an aid to self-discovery and personal reflection. The determination of which archetypes are active is a personal one. You should not let anyone tell you what archetypes are active in your life, and you should not determine archetypes for others. You can, however, have a hypothesis that improves how you relate with another individual, and you can test that theory in the laboratory of life (i.e., does a particular archetype help you relate better to a person?).

o The purposes of working with archetypes include the following:
  • Increasing self-awareness
  • Finding greater fulfillment and meaning in life
  • Improving personal, family, community, and workplace relationships
  • Expanding abilities, perspectives, and options
  • Escaping habitual archetypal patterns that have become limiting rather than empowering paths
  • Learning to be actively engaged in charting your life journey

- Most people have one or more archetypes that remain stable over time and provide a sense of core meaning and identity. Other archetypes often change and shift over time as you face new life stages and challenges.

- The journey is a spiral one, and therefore, you may experience archetypes in an order that is unique to your own journey (see figure 1.2 on page 17). In addition, each time the archetype becomes active, you may experience it at a higher or more profound level.

- The emergence of archetypes in your life is generally an unconscious process. The PMAI® instrument helps make that process conscious. Once you are aware of the archetypes that are active in your life, focused intent can help an archetype awaken, and can influence the level of the archetype's expression.

- Think of archetypes as seeds within the unconscious. These seeds receive the "sunlight" necessary for growth when you seek out people (family members, people in your ethnic group, co-workers, friends) who reinforce the archetypes you want to develop. This nurturing, along with your own conscious decisions, encourages the archetypes to "sprout." (Note that in the absence of nourishment, they may remain dormant.)

- You can also look at archetypes as sources of energy that exist in the unconscious that help you find the motivation to maximize your gifts and abilities, and to become more developed and mature. This energy can assist you in having a greater quality of life (i.e., being happier and more successful as you fulfill your potential).

- If you gained the gifts of an archetype in the past, you can retain its gifts even though its narrative pattern may no longer be dominant. Archetypes are natural to the human psyche, so they stand in waiting, available when they are needed. Pay attention as you read through the descriptors to archetypes that may have been active in your life in the past, even if their current scores are not as high. It is likely that you still have access to the gifts of these archetypes, even though they no longer give you energy or determine the flow of your life. ○

**CHAPTER 3**

# Steps for Validating
# and Understanding Your Results

o    o    o

*The Pearson-Marr Archetype Indicator® (PMAI®) assessment can help you reflect on the archetypal stories most prominent in your current life. By giving you a sense of which archetypes are dominant in your life and which ones are in the background (even disowned), the PMAI® assessment assists you in understanding the mix of stories that informs your life narrative.*

*As explained earlier in this guide, active and dominant archetypes may change from time to time depending upon your circumstances. As archetypes are not static, you may wish to retake the instrument as you progress on your journey, when you are stressed, or when you undergo major life changes, such as marriage, job change, or geographic relocation. To learn about the archetypes currently active in your life, as well as those* that may have been active in the past, you will need to refer to the archetype descriptions in chapter 8. Once you have acquainted yourself with the archetype descriptions, use the following step-by-step process to help you identity the archetypes active in your life, determine archetypes active previously in your life, and interpret your results from the PMAI® instrument.

**READ ME!**

The exercises in this chapter are designed to lead you to a deeper understanding of the archetypes and of your own life story. They are not designed to be completed at one sitting, but over time with the opportunity for reflection. Working through the exercises in a study group is a helpful way to enhance your understanding and deepen the connection with the group members.

o   o   o

## STEP ONE
### Record how the archetypes function in your life.

Refer to the Archetype Score-Ranges worksheet (page 19), where you wrote the names of your highest, lowest, and midrange archetypes. Read the meaning of their functions in your life. Then, using the scores for the archetypes, follow these steps to help validate your results:

1　*In the 24 to 30 range,* **circle** the one or two archetypes that seem to be most characteristic of you. (If you have no scores in this category, move down to your top three scores in the next range–more if you have a tie–and circle the one or two that seem most like you).

2　*In the 18 to 23 range,* put a **star** by any archetype that seems enticing to you and that you might want to have more of in your life. Put a **check mark** by any that may have been more active earlier in your life than they are now.

3　*In the 6 to 18 range,* put an **X** by any archetype that (1) reminds you of some person you find difficult or bewildering or (2) that reminds you of a situation that has been difficult for you to manage or resolve. Put a **star** by archetypes that you wish you had more of in your life.

## STEP TWO
### Validate your scores.

The PMAI® instrument is not a substitute for your own judgment. Rather, it is a mirror to help you have a conversation with yourself and others about the stories that influence your life and that create or inhibit the satisfaction you get from life. If, after reading the relevant descriptions in chapter 8, any of your scores feel inaccurate, there are several steps you can take to check them against your experience. Remember *you* get the final say about what is true for you.

1 *Put marks by archetype scores you wish to reconsider and make brief notes why.*

2 *Check your responses to the questions on the PMAI® instrument for that archetype.* Go back to your PMAI® questionnaire and read the questions and your responses to any archetype on which you scored differently than you expected. (You can do this by locating the questions by number in the column that you added for the total score for that archetype.) Try to determine if you may have read a question somewhat differently than others might. Then look back at that archetypal description to see if the archetype is dominant in your life but with a somewhat different style or expression than the questions reflect. Please note that the Destroyer scale does *not* measure the outlaw or revolutionary aspects of the Destroyer archetype. The Destroyer questions on the PMAI® instrument focus more narrowly on the experiences of loss and letting go. You may score low on this archetype if you express it as the outlaw or revolutionary.

3 *Notice whether you have a mixture of high and low scores for the archetype in question.* You may be expressing the archetype in a particular style or modality but not in others. If you think the archetype is more active than the instrument would suggest, then notice the items on which you scored low. These may describe aspects of the archetype that are not currently expressed in your life, even though the archetype, over all, is strong for you.

4 *Determine if the level of the archetype in your life is higher than that tested by the PMAI® instrument.* The questions on the PMAI® tool are most often framed at the midrange level for an archetype, tapping a mix of positive and negative aspects. Sometimes a person in whom an archetype is expressed at its highest level may score low in that category. For example, if you are a wonderfully generous, compassionate, and giving person, and you also have ease in setting boundaries, saying "no," and taking care of *yourself* as well, you may be an exemplary Caregiver. However, since most midrange Caregivers are less good at caring for themselves than for others—and the questions on the PMAI® instrument reflect this imbalance—your Caregiver score may not reflect the full strength of that archetype in your life. Use the checklist in figure 3.1 (page 30) to note the archetypes you express at *high positive* levels.

5 *Be alert to other influences.* Look back at the items for the archetype or archetypes that you question and determine if your answers genuinely reflect what you really think and feel, or if they reflect what others (partner, parent, teacher, employer) think you *should be*.

FIGURE 3.1 **Archetypes Expressed in Their Highest Levels**

| | **I embody the achieved levels of the following archetypes. (Check all that apply)** |
|---|---|
| ○ **Innocent** | I am filled with optimism and faith, but I am not prone to denial. |
| ○ **Orphan** | I am resilient, and able to anticipate and head off trouble without blaming others or myself if things do not work out. |
| ○ **Warrior** | I achieve my goals and can be tough with adversaries, but I consistently seek out win/win solutions. |
| ○ **Caregiver** | I am generous, caring, and compassionate, but I do not martyr myself or enable others' weaknesses or dependencies. |
| ○ **Seeker** | I have an independent spirit and know who I am, but I can also commit to others and be close to them. |
| ○ **Lover** | I am passionate, loving, romantic, and good at intimacy, but I am OK by myself. |
| ○ **Destroyer** | I know how to let go of what is not working and to trust something else will replace it, but I am not destructive to others or myself. |
| ○ **Creator** | I am imaginative, visionary, and skilled at manifesting my vision, but I am not a perfectionist or critical of others or myself. |
| ○ **Ruler** | I am comfortable with exerting power and authority, and I use my power for my good and that of others. |
| ○ **Magician** | I am a catalyst for healing and transformation so that both others and I experience a much better life. |
| ○ **Sage** | I am consistently curious, seeking truth, and avoiding the temptations of dogma, ivory tower irrelevance, or "anything goes" relativism. |
| ○ **Jester** | I have a great time, liven other people up, and free up possibilities; but I also meet my responsibilities and live in a healthy, responsible way. |

## STEP THREE

### Understand your high scores.

① *Determine the four archetypes that are highest for you.* Write the names of these archetypes in the spaces provided, starting with the archetype with the highest score and working down.

*Highest archetype:* _____

*Second highest archetype:* _____

*Third highest archetype:* _____

*Fourth highest archetype:* _____

These are the archetypal characters likely to be most influential in your life right now. Your leadership approaches are likely to reflect the stories of these archetypes, with their corresponding strengths, needs, aspirations, and pitfalls. See chapter 8 for detailed descriptions.

The archetypes you are living are helping you to develop their gifts. If an archetype has been active in your life for a long time, it is possible that you already have some of the qualities described in figure 3.1 on the opposite page.

2 *Review the descriptions for the strengths and pitfalls of your highest archetypes.* Refer to the description of your highest archetype in chapter 8, specifically noting the characteristics. In what way is that energy being expressed in your life right now? It surprises people sometimes to find that they exhibit both the positive and the negative qualities of an archetype. Your PMAI® results will not tell you whether you have the strengths or the pitfalls of the archetype (see figures 2.1 and 2.2, as well as the individual descriptions of the archetypes for details). The scores tell you *how strongly* the archetype affects your life, not whether it does so in a positive or negative way or at what level it is expressed. List the strengths and pitfalls of your highest archetypes that are most applicable in your current life.

*Highest Archetype* _____

| Strengths you recognize in yourself | Pitfalls you recognize in yourself |
|---|---|
|  |  |
|  |  |
|  |  |

Remember that negative archetypal qualities can be redirected into more positive expressions. You do this by paying attention to what you are thinking and doing and consciously choosing not to act out the negative possibility, experimenting instead with more positive expressions of that energy.

Make notes here about shifts from negative expressions to positive ones that you would like to make:

_____

_____

_____

_____

_____

(3) *Assess whether the expression of the archetype feels empowering or limiting.* Most of the time the archetypes active in your life feel empowering because they give you energy and encourage skills and activities that are right for you at this time. Such archetypal expressions offer resources that can help you develop new skills and excel in ways you never thought possible. However, there are a few ways that your archetypes can trip you up:

- Your archetypal gifts may make you think that you are better than others. This is called inflation. A clue to inflation is to observe if you feel empty, depleted, or even deflated (like the air going out of a balloon) when that particular archetype expression is over. For example, a person giving a well-received talk may feel extremely wise (Sage archetype), like a guru or oracle. However, later in the hotel room, he or she may suddenly feel vulnerable and needy.

An archetype can also take you over, so you either live out its story compulsively (for example, a person expressing Caregiver who can never say "no," or someone expressing Ruler who cannot be comfortable when not in control). This is called archetypal possession or archetypal trance.

- Archetypes also can become stereotypes. If you cling to a particular archetypal expression so much that you and others expect that expression, you may become too rigid in that role. Inside you, new archetypes are ready to emerge, but the combination of habit and pressure from others' expectations can lock you into an old way of being. You can tell that this has happened if you are doing things that once made you happy, but you observe that you are becoming bored and unhappy. The answer is to allow the expression of emerging archetypes to help rekindle your joy in life.

Make notes of ways your active archetypes are empowering or limiting in the roles you play:

*Empowering* _____

_____

_____

*Limiting* _____

_____

_____

**4** *Understand the energies of your highest archetypes and whether they are expressed in integrated or conflicted ways.*

*Integrated combinations.* If you scored equally (or almost equally) high on two or more archetypes, they may inform your life story in a way that is *combined and integrated.* In this case, there is a good possibility that both archetypal themes are active in your life. For example, Tom scored almost the same on Warrior as on Lover; and these were his two highest scores. Tom had a life-long passion for trains. He loved to collect model trains and to sculpt scenes and railroad beds. He attended auctions where he was an aggressive and successful bidder for model railroad paraphernalia. In his career, he was a manager of a government agency over-seeing the effectiveness of transportation. He took his job seriously (perhaps a bit too seriously according to some colleagues), working tirelessly for transportation safety and efficiency. He combined the passion of the Lover with the focus, aggression, and attention to detail typical of the Warrior.

Take a moment to make notes here about ways your highest archetypes work well together.

_____

_____

_____

_____

*Conflicted combinations.* Sometimes when a person scores highest on two or more archetypes, the archetypal characters may be in conflict in his or her story. Laura had been offered a much sought after managerial position in a firm shortly after completing law school. At the same time, she learned that she was pregnant. She took the job, feeling more and more pressured as her energy waned in the latter months of the pregnancy, and she was faced with declaring how soon she might return to work following the birth. Her two high scores of Warrior and Caregiver presaged the climax of an internal battle that caused her much suffering. Finally recognizing that neither archetypal expression was going to be silenced or "go away," she gave expression to both by writing a dialogue between the two archetypes in her journal. Her Warrior came to realize that it was her child who needed protecting; her Warrior energy had been directed in support of performing her career instead of creating a safe environment for her baby. With this realization she met with her boss and was fully prepared to resign the new position. Instead her boss arranged for her to job share for a year until she felt she could comfortably engage child care. Laura's story is an example of how often, when the internal dispute is voiced, the external events fall into place.

Similarly, John's Caregiver was so strong it always shouted down his Seeker, so he took care of others rather than exploring what was possible for him. As a result, he always felt unfulfilled and occasionally resentful of what he saw as others' demands. It was only after a severe bout of mononucleosis that demanded almost a year's convalescence that he slowly began pursuing his early love of old-time music. As he recovered he began traveling to music festivals throughout the country and, later, the world. Still a caring person, he found he was more often joyful and rarely resentful.

Describe a situation in your life where you say you want to do something, but do not do it.

_____

_____

_____

_____

_____

_____

_____

_____

How might you experiment with living out this story at least in small ways?

_____

_____

_____

_____

_____

_____

_____

_____

Think of the parts of you that want to succeed in accomplishing your goal and those that resist. Give them archetypal names. What archetypes are involved and what role does each play in your life?

_____

_____

_____

_____

_____

_____

If any of these roles are in conflict, how might they be reconciled?

_____

_____

_____

_____

_____

_____

## STEP FOUR

### Find your dominant life story.

Think back to the story of *Little Mouse*; we will use the same way of thinking to look at the setting, tone, characters, and plot structure that are present in the events in your life. First, we will look at the archetypal life myth or story that was present in your growing up years. Often this original life story informs your current life, just with more complexity or in a more mature fashion.

Then we will explore the archetypal story that informs your current life using a process similar to the one we just used in exploring your childhood myth. You will be able to see how the two are related in forming your overall life story.

## Your Personal Childhood Myth

**Setting:** Describe the major life setting in which you spent the majority of your childhood time (for many, it's likely to be your home, your school, or the home of a relative or friend). Consider this the setting of your story. Write the name of that setting here:

_____

**Characters:** The earliest ideas of the characters in your life story come from the people around you, usually family. List the important people with whom you lived in your early growing up years, such as parents, step parents, brothers, sisters, and step siblings. If there was someone else who lived with you, or with whom you lived, include them as well (e.g., a grandmother with whom you spent summers or an uncle who lived with your family). Try to think of family members from before the third grade, if possible. Be sure to include yourself. (You may have only one or two family-member characters in your plot, or you may have many. Try to keep the list to the important family members who had the most influence on your story.) On the line beside each, write which of the twelve archetypes each character seems most influenced by, and the gift that archetype brings. Next, write any of the archetypal pitfalls those characters seem to express.

| People | Major Archetype | Gift Expressed | Pitfall Expressed |
|---|---|---|---|
| 1) | | | |
| 2) | | | |
| 3) | | | |
| 4) | | | |
| 5) | | | |
| 6) | | | |
| 7) | | | |
| 8) | | | |
| 9) | | | |
| 10) | | | |

**Tone:** In one to three words, how would you describe the emotional climate, the atmosphere or tone of your childhood family (for example, empowering, tense, distant, or easy going)? Write the tone here: _____

**Plot:** To understand the overall plot of your childhood story, it is easiest to combine the plots of several childhood events or stories. In the space provided write separate brief vignettes describing three memorable stories about yourself from childhood.

The *first story* should be your earliest memory. Don't labor over which episode is earliest, just choose one that comes to mind.

The *second story* should be the family story about your birth; or, if you do not know the story of your birth, choose a family story about your infancy or early childhood.

The *third story* should be your favorite childhood story from a fairy tale, a children's book, a movie, or a TV program.

The vignettes should be specific, containing a sequence of events, actions, or conversations that involved people important to you in the setting you have chosen. If you do not like to write, just make an outline or enough notes for you to decode the plot or the story you are telling.

1 *Vignette of your earliest memory:*

_____

_____

_____

_____

_____

_____

_____

_____

What feelings, if any, are contained in the story or evoked by the story?

_____

_____

_____

_____

_____

(2) *Vignette of your birth or infancy story:*

_____

_____

_____

_____

_____

_____

_____

_____

What feelings, if any, are contained in the story or evoked by the story?

_____

_____

_____

_____

_____

(3) *Vignette of your favorite childhood story:*

_____

_____

_____

_____

_____

_____

_____

_____

What feelings, if any, are contained in the story or evoked by the story?

_____

_____

_____

_____

_____

_____

_____

_____

_____

_____

_____

**Plot summaries:** A plot is a sequence of events often marked by a series of actions. One character says or does something, another responds, and so on. The plot usually builds to a climax and then moves to a turning point (called a _denouement_), which ends the suspense. For many people, the same plots recur, and shorter or smaller events may have similar patterns to the main story. In the following chart, summarize the childhood vignettes you wrote about. Then write a headline for the story in the same manner that an editor would write a headline for a newspaper story.

_Story One_

_Earliest Memory_ _____

_____

_____

_Title (Headline)_ _____

_Archetype (Which archetype's plot is the story most like?)_ _____

_____

*Story Two*

*Birth or Infancy Story* _____

_____

*Title (headline)* _____

*Archetype (What archetype's plot is this story most like?)* _____

_____

*Story Three*

*Favorite Childhood Story* _____

_____

*Title (headline)* _____

*Archetype (What archetype's plot is this story most like?)* _____

_____

Review the titles and summaries of the three childhood stories. What is the major combined theme of the vignettes? Theme:

_____

## Your Current Personal Story

**Setting:** While the childhood setting was a family, your predominant current setting may be work, school, home, or friendship. Describe the major life setting in which you spend the majority of your time (for many, it's likely to be your work, your home, or your school). Consider this the setting of your story. Write the name of that setting here:

_____

**Tone:** In one to three words, how would you describe the emotional climate, the atmosphere, or tone of that setting (for example, empowering, tense, distant, or easy going)? Write the tone here:

_____

**Characters:** List the important people in this setting. Be sure to include yourself. (Again, you may have only one or two people/characters in your plot, or you may have many.) Try to keep the list to the important people who have the most influence on your story. On the line beside each, write which of the twelve archetypes each character seems most influenced by, and the gift that archetype brings. Next, write any of the archetypal pitfalls those characters seem to express.

| People | Major Archetype | Gift Expressed | Pitfall Expressed |
|---|---|---|---|
| 1) | | | |
| 2) | | | |
| 3) | | | |
| 4) | | | |
| 5) | | | |
| 6) | | | |
| 7) | | | |
| 8) | | | |
| 9) | | | |
| 10) | | | |

**Plot:** To understand the overall plot of your current life story, it is easiest to combine the plots of several events or stories just as we did for your childhood myth. This time we will use only two stories. In the space provided, write separate brief vignettes describing two memorable stories about yourself in the setting that you selected. The first should be about a satisfying time, a time when you felt you were at your best. The second should be about a troubling time when you did not feel at your best. Don't labor over which events to record; just choose two that come to mind.

1 *Vignette of a satisfying, fulfilling, or effective time:*

_____

_____

_____

_____

_____

_____

_____

_____

_____

_____

_____

_____

_____

**2** *Vignette of a troubling time:*

_____

_____

_____

_____

_____

_____

_____

_____

_____

**Plot summaries:** As noted previously, a plot is a sequence of events often marked by a series of actions—one character says or does something, another responds, and so on. The plot usually builds to a climax and then moves to a turning point, which ends the suspense. For many people, the same plots recur, and shorter or smaller events may have similar patterns to the main story. Summarize briefly in the following chart the vignettes you wrote about occurring in your dominant setting. And then write a headline for the story in the same manner that an editor would write a headline for a newspaper story.

*Story One*

*Fulfilling Time* _____

_____

_____

*Title (Headline)* _____

*Archetype (Which archetype's plot is the story most like?)* _____

_____

*Story Two*

*Troubling Time* _____

_____

_____

*Title (headline)* _____

*Archetype (What archetype's plot is this story most like?)* _____

_____

Review the headlines, archetypes, and summaries of the two current myth vignettes. What is the major combined theme of the vignettes? Theme:

_____

_____

_____

_____

How does this compare with the theme of your childhood myth? How might the plots and themes combine?

_____

_____

_____

Review your titles, plots, and feelings for the combined theme. Then, in the following space, write the major combined plot.

_____

_____

_____

_____

_____

Do most of these scenarios cluster around one archetypal narrative? If so, briefly summarize that archetypal story. If there are several different archetypal stories, what are they?

_____

_____

_____

_____

_____

_____

_____

_____

_____

_____

If you have identified one primary archetypal story, this may be your life myth, in which case you may find that your life is enhanced by committing more fully to that story and its possibilities. If you have identified several, live each consciously until it becomes obvious which seems most authentic and fulfilling to you.

Alternative endings: There are many versions of each story and so the endings of similar plots may vary. Consider what you might change in your childhood myth and/or in your current story to be more successful and fulfilled. Use the following space to retell the stories the way you wish they would happen–in the present tense, as if that is how it is.

*Story One*

_____

_____

_____

_____

_____

*Story Two*

_____

_____

_____

_____

## STEP FIVE
### Understand your low scores.

You may be primarily interested in understanding your high scores and learning how the dominant archetypes affect your life. However, you may choose to examine areas of your life that are affected by archetypes that are *not* available to you. Sometimes having access to different stories may help you overcome difficulties, address conflict, and/or move forward in your life. The following analysis can help you understand the archetypes for which you scored low.

**1** *List the two archetypes on which you scored lowest and then read about them in chapter 8:*

_____

_____

There are several ways to understand low scores, and it is important to think through which may be most applicable. The low scores on your graph may represent characteristic ways of organizing the world that do not currently apply to you; or ones which you have not yet encountered in yourself. It is possible you may have difficulty working with people who are living your low-scoring archetypal stories. You may also have difficulty in situations that require the gifts and perspectives of these lower scoring archetypes.

(2) *Establish if any of your own scores are dormant, shadow, or "allergy."* There may be many reasons why you scored low on certain archetypes. Following are three explanations for why your scores might be low and hints about how to determine which one applies to your situation. You will want to know if the archetypes on which you scored low have never been needed, are disowned parts of the self, or are parts that have previously taken you over. (In general that determination is made by the amount of emotional energy invested.)

- Your low-scored archetypes may indicate that you have not needed these particular archetypes because you have not yet faced their challenges. You can think of these unencountered archetypes as *dormant.* An unencountered or dormant archetype generates little energy. You may find the descriptions somewhat foreign, and your reaction is likely to be unemotional and disinterested.

- The low-scored archetypes may reflect those characteristics that you actively disown in yourself. If this is the case, these archetypes may represent your alter ego or shadow self, of which others may be more aware than you are. Reclaiming these disowned parts of yourself may provide you with more choices for responding to situations and may make it less likely that you will be unaware of your own actions or feelings. This reclamation is a step toward further personal growth.

- If the archetype is a shadow aspect, you are likely to be more energetic, even adamant that this is *not* an influence in your life. You may think of people influential in your life who *do* exhibit aspects of this archetype, and you are likely to have a negative reaction to it. Because it is disowned, the archetype is more likely to be expressed in its less differentiated and more problematic aspects. If you have friends who can be forthright with you, ask them, "In what ways do I show (list the positive and negative aspects of the archetype)?"

- The archetypes on which you scored low may represent qualities that you have overused in the past and need to stay away from. One woman, for example, had been such a Caregiver in her family and in her nursing career that she no longer even wanted to water her plants. We call this an allergy. Overexposure to an archetype may make its expression toxic.

- It may be quite obvious to you if an archetype is an allergy. You will know it well but feel an aversion that is something like, "Oh, not again!" You also may feel annoyed at people you know who overexpress that archetype, and in the process realize that your source of annoyance is your own frustration at overexpression of the very same archetype.

o    o    o

In the following spaces, make some notes about how you might express the low scoring archetypes in your life.

*Dormant Archetype(s):*_____

_____

*Shadow Archetype(s):*_____

_____

*Allergy Archetype(s):* _____

_____

(3) *Assess situations or relationships that are difficult for you in light of low scores.* Recognizing your low scores is important when you are in a situation that seems as if it is defeating you. Often, if you do not know what to do to make it better, you either ignore it or obsess about it. You may encounter such situations because you do not have access to the gifts of the archetype that could help you know how to handle this difficulty.

List two situations that are currently troubling to you:

_____

_____

Review figure 2.1 (The Archetypal Gifts) and use the chart to record the gifts of your low archetypes. (You may also review the archetype descriptions in chapter 8 to look for more ideas of the gifts of the archetypes on which you scored low.) Note the ways you may be able to use those gifts.

| Low archetypes | Gifts | How would this gift be helpful? |
|---|---|---|
|  |  |  |
|  |  |  |
|  |  |  |

You can increase an archetype's availability to you by using the following techniques:

- Recognize its value and decide that the archetype would be a good one for you to express.

- Read books, watch movies, listen to music, and view art that reflect the archetype.

- Be around people who express the archetype in its positive forms.

- Consciously act, dress, speak, and think as that archetype does.

- Consider when in your life you decided that particular story would not be appropriate for you. Be open to making a new decision about that archetype. (Ask yourself who dissuaded you from living that story or expressing the attributes of that archetype. Also review who in your life might have lived that story so badly that you decided *not* to be like them.)

4 *Recognize any tendency to project your shadow archetype(s) onto others.* Your low scores can cause you to be more intolerant of others, especially those who express the common pitfalls of the archetypes you most want to avoid. You may find it helpful to actually write the names of people you find particularly annoying or troubling. You can also include people you do not personally know, such as celebrities; politicians; newsmakers; and even characters from books, movies, or TV shows. Note what is so annoying about them and check these against the common pitfalls for that archetype. What archetypes do they represent? Is there a relationship to your low scores?

| Annoying people | Annoying qualities | Archetype |
|---|---|---|
| | | |
| | | |
| | | |

What is the cost to you of not relating well to people with these qualities?

_____

_____

You may find that you are more understanding of difficult people when you recognize which archetypes are being expressed (although it may be the negative aspects), and you may begin to notice occasions on which those archetypes are expressed positively.

**5** *Examine your life stages and situations.* There are particular life stages and situations that are difficult if certain archetypes are not yet available to you. For example, it is difficult to be a new parent without some access to an inner Caregiver or to be a soldier going to war without some access to the inner Warrior. On the following chart, circle any archetype on which you scored low, but that you need because of the life stage or situation in which you currently find yourself.

| Archetype | Typical Situation | Typical Life Stage* |
| --- | --- | --- |
| Innocent | Safe, secure place and time | Childhood |
| Orphan | Powerlessness, betrayal | Childhood |
| Seeker | On one's own, independence | Adolescence |
| Lover | Love relationship or close friendship | Adolescence |
| Warrior | Challenge to fight or meet goals | Adulthood |
| Caregiver | Responsibility to care for others | Adulthood |
| Destroyer | Time of loss or need to clear out | Midlife |
| Creator | Need to create something new | Midlife |
| Ruler | Positional authority | Post-midlife |
| Magician | Power to influence others | Post-midlife |
| Sage | Need to understand something | Retirement |
| Jester | Vacation, recreation, relaxing | Retirement |

*Please note that the archetypes can be expressed at any life stage, but in a linear expression of journey, the archetypes are most commonly experienced at the life stages described in the chart.*

Notes: _____

_____

_____

## STEP SIX

### Expand your options.

People are often limited in their outlook because they think, feel, and act in habitual patterns that arise from the archetypes. In order to practice moving beyond the selective focus of your dominant archetypes, pick one issue in your life that feels challenging to you: something that you do not know how to handle or that you feel you are not handling well or that is not going well. You may expand your options in either an extraverted or an introverted manner, depending upon which seems to fit best for you.

**1** *Describe the problem in one of the two following ways:*

A) *Extraverted Option*

Explain the problem to another person, then summarize the essence here:

_____

_____

_____

_____

_____

B) *Introverted Option*

Describe the problem in the space provided here:

_____

_____

_____

_____

_____

_____

_____

_____

_____

_____

Summarize the essence of the problem:

_____

_____

_____

Continue with the following steps regardless of which option you chose.

**2** *Describe briefly how you have grappled with the problem or how you might ordinarily react.*

**3** *Identify the archetype(s) reflected in your response.*

Archetype: _____

Archetype: _____

Archetype: _____

If you chose the extraverted option, role-play with one other person who plays in turn the part of each of the three archetypes you listed. If you chose the introverted option, write a dialogue with the archetypes you have listed.

**4** *Summarize the advice that can be garnered from how these archetypes act in the situation you set up.* You can do this through additional role-play or written dialogue. Remember that you and others have all the archetypes within you, so you can access their wisdom. However, it is easier to do so if you lighten up and do this in the spirit of play.

_____

_____

_____

_____

_____

_____

_____

**5** *Given these new perspectives, what might you do differently?*

_____

_____

_____

_____

_____

_____

_____

You may wish to repeat this exercise on additional paper, using a different issue or challenge. You can also use this exercise to examine past issues in order to think through what might have been, to explore present issues to expand your horizons, or to consider your actions for future situations.

## STEP SEVEN

### Sum up your PMAI® results and self–analysis.

It is useful after undertaking the detailed analysis included in this chapter to sum up your results. Doing so helps you retain what you have learned about yourself as well as what you have decided to do with that knowledge. Complete the *Summary Chart of PMAI® Results* using the guidelines provided. (Remember, if you have determined that your PMAI® results are imprecise in some way, correct for this, using your own judgment about what is true for you.)

**READ ME!**

### Guidelines for completing the Summary Chart of PMAI® Results

1) **Fill in your highest archetypes in order, beginning with the highest score.**

2) **Write down your lowest archetypes.**

3) **Describe the quality of each archetype's expression, for example, empowering (gifts) or limiting (dormant, shadow, allergy). Next, look over the following actions and use the symbol to mark the appropriate archetypes.**

   o **Circle** the archetype that most closely approximates the dominant story pattern in your life.

   o **Underline** the archetype you think might be true of a deeper part of you that you would like to express in your life.

   o Use a **plus sign** (+) to mark any archetypes you would like more of.

   o Use a **minus sign** (–) to mark any archetypes you would like less of.

   o Place an **arrow** by any archetype that you believe might be more of an ally for you if you expressed it in more positive ways.

4) **Summarize your insights and the changes you plan to make in the spaces provided following the chart.**

o o o

## Summary Chart of PMAI® Results

| Highest archetypes | | Quality of expression |
|---|---|---|
| 1) | | |
| 2) | | |
| 3) | | |
| 4) | | |

| Lowest archetypes | | Quality of expression |
|---|---|---|
| 1) | | |
| 2) | | |

*Insights* _____

_____

_____

_____

_____

_____

_____

_____

_____

*Desired changes* _____

_____

_____

_____

_____

_____

_____

_____

_____

# NOTES

**CHAPTER 4**

# Living the Hero's Journey with Consciousness

o   o   o

*Archetypal stories of heroes and heroines in all cultures help us understand the ideal for how we live. These archetypal stories provide the call to live life at a new level. The results from your Pearson-Marr Archetype Indicator® (PMAI®) assessment make it possible for you to understand and explore how archetypal stories influence your life. In addition to the analyses you have undertaken thus far, you can use what you have learned about yourself to see where you are in the three major stages of the hero's journey. The hero's journey is one way to understand the individuation process—that is, the journey to finding your uniqueness and learning to express your highest potential in positive ways in your life, family, community, and work. The pattern of living these stories is unique to each individual. The journey* described here is in a linear form because it is easier to understand, but your personal journey is more likely to be experienced in a spiral way, which will be discussed further at the end of this chapter. This spiral concept is important because we constantly circle back to relive archetypal narratives, and each time our experience of the possibilities within any given story deepens (refer to figure 1.2).

Each of the twelve stories described in this book can be seen as a part of the larger narrative of the hero's journey and leading to a heroic gift. All the stories require courage, even though, for example, the courage of the Warrior (to fight to achieve goals) and the courage of the Lover (to let down barriers to be completely seen and known) differ profoundly. Recognizing which archetypes are active in your life right now is a way of discovering what heroic challenge or challenges you may be facing. Putting your life within this context ennobles what may seem like everyday problems and triumphs and connects your trials, tribulations, and exultations to the great heroes of all times. This process can help you to become a more mature, fully realized human being.

The hero's journey is the overarching story that prepares us to take on the responsibilities of adulthood and citizenship. This may involve exercising individual responsibility (as a parent, a boss, a community leader, a political office holder) and/or participating in shared responsibilities (as a voter, a concerned citizen, a member of a work or volunteer team, a responsible family member).

While stories of heroes in myths, legends, and fairy tales ordinarily seem removed from our everyday lives, we can see some of their patterns as we examine our own archetypal stories. Noticing the stages of the hero's journey can help us claim the nobility of our own lives, even during life's most difficult passages.

Each of the archetypes presides over a stage in the heroic journey. Within the larger pattern of the twelve stages of the hero's journey, there are three intermediate journeys, each of which is aided by four of the archetypal narratives described in this book.

*The Preparation for the Journey*: Innocent, Orphan, Caregiver, and Warrior (associated with the ego level of development)

*The Transformational Journey*: Seeker, Destroyer, Lover, Creator (associated with the soul level of development)

*The Return from the Journey*: Ruler, Magician, Sage, Jester (associated with the self level of development)

Each of the stages gives you gifts, and each has its traps–traps that are more difficult to avoid if you are not able to anticipate and recognize them.

Before reading about each of these stages, complete the Stages of Your Heroic Journey worksheet (page 59) by recording the scores for each of your archetypes and then adding the scores for each group. If any one of the sums is significantly higher than the others, you may be focusing your energy primarily in that phase of the journey (preparation, journey, or return).

o   o   o

## The Three Stages of the Hero's Journey

### *The Preparation for the Journey*

We prepare for the journey by awakening the four archetypes that provide us with an inner family (Innocent, Orphan, Warrior, Caregiver), thus freeing us from issues determined by our family of origin. The stories associated with the preparation are related to this inner family: the Innocent and the Orphan are two sides of the inner child (spontaneous and wounded); and the Caregiver and the Warrior are two sides of the inner parent (nurturing and protecting).

Living these stories helps us with good ego development. The open, receptive nature of the Innocent helps us learn and socialize. The hard knocks experienced by the Orphan help us to be appropriately cautious, realistic, and aware of our own vulnerabilities and those of others. Together these stories teach us to be discerning and resilient. Similarly, the compassionate Caregiver helps us to share with others and be nurturing and gentle with them, while the Warrior helps us to be disciplined and tough enough to set and achieve goals and create and protect boundaries. Together these archetypes help us balance getting what we want with showing kindness and consideration to others.

If your highest scores (on the Heroic Journey worksheet) are in the preparation stage, it means you are working on issues related to dealing with the vulnerabilities of being human and also learning to grapple with those difficulties in a way that is socially acceptable in the society in which you live.

You can see the pattern of development of these four archetypes in fairy tales, albeit communicated in metaphorical terms. In the beginning, the hero has the virtues of the Innocent because he has the optimism to begin the journey. Along the way, he has to distinguish between tempters and guides, thus requiring him to balance the Innocent with the skepticism of the Orphan. At some point, he meets a dragon or other monster that he must slay (Warrior), proving he has strength and courage, and someone in need he must help (Caregiver). In many stories, the hero meets an old man or woman who has nothing. The hero also has little, but he shares gladly what he has, demonstrating that he is not just out for himself. He cares about other human beings, showing he has a wise and noble enough heart to take the journey.

When we experience these four archetypes in trance forms (discussed in chapter 2), we may demonstrate the qualities that are often identified with the negative aspects of the ego. From a psychological perspective, the ego's positive function is to keep us safe, differentiate us from others, and give us a sense of individual worth. So, when we overdo this, as happens in the trance state, we may become fearful and lonely, and, in order to protect our sense of worth (ego), we may make excuses or blame others when we make mistakes.

Then all of life becomes a way to keep the vulnerable inner child safe as the world is imagined as a treacherous place. The Innocent desperately seeks to please, the Orphan uses the victim role to manipulate others, the Warrior preemptively attacks, and the Caregiver obsessively rescues others.

The antidotes to this dilemma, which can happen naturally as we experience more and more of life, are to learn how the world works (so you know when you are safe and when not); to gain the emotional intelligence to recognize when you should trust and when you should not; and to develop your Warrior strength and your Caregiver ability to care for yourself and others, so that you develop inner parents to protect, nurture, and coach your inner child. In addition, you are much less likely to experience the ego archetypes in their trance forms if you have taken your soul journey, so that you find an identity deeper than the ego.

## The Transformational Journey

Following the preparation, we begin to experience the journey. The four archetypes that help with the journey (Seeker, Lover, Destroyer, Creator) preside over a transformation process. The journey can begin with the Seeker's curiosity about the self and the world or a pervasive sense of boredom, emptiness, and dissatisfaction. It also can begin with the experience of loss, when people and things are taken from us or when our ego-defenses are undermined or when we are brought face to face with ways in which we have failed to live up to our ideals (Destroyer). Either way, we step out to explore, and in the process let go of what is no longer relevant in our lives. In the first instance, we are motivated by hopes for the future and discover we cannot have a new life without sacrificing some of the old; whereas, in the second, we are moved to seek because much has been taken from us. Either way the initiation of the journey usually entails some suffering or loss.

Although we are ultimately questing for self-knowledge, the conscious motivation of the journey is often to find ourselves and feel at home (or to reclaim that feeling if we have been forced out of what seemed to be a safe haven or personal Eden). In this process, we find who we are through the various expressions of the archetypes active in this stage. We do this in part by what we let go of and in part by what we find that we love (Lover)–people, places, activities–and by what we create in our lives and work (Creator). When we create from the

# Worksheet: Stages of Your Heroic Journey

......... **1** .........

| Innocent | Orphan | Warrior | Caregiver | *Preparation* |
|---|---|---|---|---|
| SCORE | SCORE | SCORE | SCORE | Sum |
| | + | + | + | = |

......... **2** .........

| Seeker | Destroyer | Lover | Creator | *Journey* |
|---|---|---|---|---|
| SCORE | SCORE | SCORE | SCORE | Sum |
| | + | + | + | = |

......... **3** .........

| Ruler | Magician | Sage | Jester | *Return* |
|---|---|---|---|---|
| SCORE | SCORE | SCORE | SCORE | Sum |
| | + | + | + | = |

level of the soul–which we do when we are living our purpose–instead of just from the ego, our lives begin to fit and satisfy us.

In mythic stories of the hero's journey, the hero embarks on a great adventure (Seeker), experiences difficulty and suffering (Destroyer) as well as love of life, of individuals, of causes, or places (Lover), which can mitigate the aspects of the Destroyer. Ultimately, the hero demonstrates resourcefulness and imagination in finding the way and solutions to obstacles (Creator), and eventually a treasure emerges (one's own gifts and nature).

In the trance version of this story, people will wander aimlessly, never finding themselves, develop self-destructive habits or do things that harm others, create endless dramas in their lives that divert them from their real creativity, and give in to self-indulgent pleasures, rather than committing to real love. The antidote, in all these situations, is to confront one's own soul and live out one's own destiny, however difficult doing so might be.

### The Return from the Journey

The challenge of the *return* is to share your talents and gifts with the world, once you have found them. Classically, at the close of the hero's journey, the hero comes back to the kingdom and becomes the king or queen. Thus, the archetypal stories associated with this challenge are those associated with the royal court and the archetypes of the Ruler, the Magician, the Sage, and the Jester. We find stories about the return generally in legends or histories about extraordinary leaders, who, like King Arthur, took the risk to serve out of a commitment to the greater good. In our own lives, we can feel royal when we are both true to ourselves and committed to sharing our gifts with the world.

When you know who you are at a deeper, soul level, your Ruler instills the responsibility to live out your purpose for the greater good of the world; your Magician helps you shift consciousness to transform or heal; your Sage is curious to know the real truth, to share wisdom respectfully with receptive and open minds; and your Jester celebrates the joy of existence in a way that is contagious and helps others enjoy themselves.

If your highest score is in the return category, it is likely that you are concerned with issues of how to share your genuine gifts with the world. If you run into problems it may be just that this stage is new to you, or that you did not first complete the work of the transformational journey. If you jump to the return without having taken the journey, these archetypes are inevitably expressed in limited or negative forms. The Ruler can be self-serving and controlling; the Magician manipulative, the Sage opinionated, and the Jester irresponsible.

Also, if you enter this stage focused only on your own good, you may become stuck in the trance version of the story. Here, the Ruler motivates a compulsive drive for power.

The Magician puts a spin on truth to distort public perception. The Sage tries to be smarter than everyone else in order to be more successful than they are. And the Jester escapes all this by pursuing mindless pleasures or conspicuous consumption. Understanding the archetypal nature of the hero's journey, therefore, is especially critical for various types of leaders–parents, advocates, community leaders, teachers, politicians, public servants, CEOs, or any other group that influences the shape of events and people's lives.

The antidote for a stuck return story is connecting with a genuine desire to be of service to the world. Each of the four self archetypes brings a gift back to the kingdom: the Ruler brings direction and organization, the Magician brings the importance of perspective, the Sage brings wisdom, and the Jester brings the ability to maintain equilibrium. These are the gifts which the Self passes on to the next generation of heroes.

o o o
## A Spiral Journey

The three stages of the journey do not ordinarily happen in a neat, linear order. You may find elements of all three in different aspects of your life at the same time, or you may look back over your life and notice a recurring pattern of getting ready, journeying to find yourself, and returning to share what you know and what you have. If you have been at the return stage and find you are again at the preparation or journey stage, it does not necessarily mean you have regressed. It means that you have more work to do on developing an even stronger and healthier ego (preparation) or a deeper, more authentic sense of soul (journey) to go to the next level of claiming your power (self) and freedom (return). Thus we revisit the preparation, journey, and return multiple times. With each new journey and return, we learn to express the archetypes in a richer and more mature fashion. This is the spiral nature of encountering the archetypes.

In fact, all three stages might be present in a single event. Let's say you are making a presentation to a client. At the ego (preparation) level, you are anxious to prove yourself. At the soul (journey) level, you are eager to do the work in a way that is authentic for you and that reflects your gifts. At the self (return) level, you want the outcome of your efforts to serve the greater good of the organization, community, nation, or world. As you begin to notice which area has the greatest resonance for you, you will begin to realize that is where your consciousness primarily lies. Within each of the three areas, the archetypal stories that score highest for you provide the narrative that most strongly energizes how you face the challenges of each of these three major and larger stages.

o    o    o

## Facing the Challenges of Modern Life

Writing about the challenges of modern life, the Harvard psychologist Robert Kegan, in his book *In Over Our Heads,* says that virtually all of us are in over our heads, because we lack the cognitive complexity to thrive in a contemporary context. What is required, he explains, is the capacity to understand and balance the following:

- an attitude of self-awareness and self-reflectiveness that allows you to think about your own thinking and analyze why you think and feel as you do,

- an ability to step out of yourself to see how it is that someone else sees something differently from you or wants something different from what you want,

- the capacity to understand organizations and other social systems and recognize their logic and their needs, and

- clear values that allow you to face the conflicts and contradictions inherent in organizational systems and decide what to do in complex and ambiguous situations.

Similarly, Daniel Goleman, in *Emotional Intelligence*, tells us that emotional intelligence is more important to success than IQ (intelligence quotient). Successful people have a capacity for personal mastery that comes from taking the time to learn to feel their feelings without having to act them out. They also foster the ability to understand others, seeking to communicate non-judgmentally and find common ground.

Understanding the stories you and others are living is a way of enhancing your cognitive complexity and emotional intelligence so that you can thrive even in today's complex times. Communications coach Arthur Cross teaches people to move from a clear articulation of "my story" and "your story" to find "our story," and thus an outcome that works for both. In a family or workplace setting, you may notice what story people are collectively living and recognize if it works for everyone, exploring the possibility of finding a new "our story" that brings a greater sense of aliveness and vitality to all involved. Because many people are trapped in stories that no longer fit, the ultimate purpose of the PMAI is to encourage you to live the stories that will help you realize your real potential as a human being.

o    o    o

## Analyzing Your Heroic Journey

Review your scores for the stages of the preparation, the journey, and the return and explore the ways the three patterns (which include the interaction of each of the four archetypes) are expressed in your life. A low score in one of the four in each stage may mean a missing character in your inner script for living out this heroic theme. For example, if most of your high scores are in the preparation stage, but your Warrior score is low, you may spend most of your time pleasing others. The antidote would be to work on calling up your Warrior, so you can become more assertive to protect your boundaries and meet your own goals. Complete the following information to help analyze the stages of your journey:

Note your positive expressions of the four-archetype combination for each stage:
(See figure 2.1 on page 22):

_____

_____

_____

Note your negative expressions of the four-archetype combination for each stage:
(See figure 2.2 on page 25):

_____

_____

_____

Note if you need to develop a missing or underdeveloped archetype to fulfill the potential of one of the four combined archetype stories:

_____

_____

_____

Make notes about any patterns you might like to enhance or change:

_____

_____

_____

You may find it helpful to combine this analysis with the analysis completed in the prior chapter as a background to writing your life story from an archetypal perspective. You do this by writing a short autobiography that references the universal stories that are active in various life situations and stages as well as noting the overall narrative of your life. You can also draw on the examples of myths and folk tales used in this book, writing your own story as if it is a myth or fairy tale, beginning with phrases like "Long ago and far away, there was a–" or "Once upon a time–" Alternative creative ways to express the universal stories you are and have been living are to paint, dance, sing, or act them out (in a one-person show or with others who play the other key characters in your life). If you observe that continuing your current life pattern might lead to outcomes you do not desire, you can also experiment with rewriting your story or otherwise expressing *alternative* versions of the same archetypal stories (what your story would look like if one or more additional archetypes were introduced or expressed at a higher level). Use the space here to begin making notes for your autobiography.

_____

_____

_____

_____

_____

_____

_____

_____

_____

_____

_____

_____

_____

_____

_____

_____

_____

CHAPTER 5

# Using Archetypes with Families, Friends, and Work Teams

o   o   o

*Inevitably, people who take the Pearson-Marr Archetype Indicator® (PMAI®)*

*instrument start thinking about how great it would be if their spouse,*

*mother, father, boss, best friend (and any number of other people) could*

*also take it. Once we recognize the power of a tool for self-discovery, it is*

*natural to want to share it with others. Moreover, when we understand the*

*archetypes, we can let go of a good bit of judgment about other people. We*

*understand they are not wrong, just because they see the world through*

*the lens of a different narrative. Helping people understand this not only*

*increases their tolerance, it also can free them from feeling upset about what*

*you and others do and say. The result could be a more peaceful world. It is* often enjoyable and enlightening to take the PMAI® instrument in a group or with members of your family or work team. (The instrument is available online and in a self-scorable, paper-and-pencil form from the publisher, the Center for Applications of Psychological Type. Visit www.capt.org for more information.) If you plan to work with groups using the PMAI® instrument or if you wish to use it in a professional capacity, the authors strongly recommend that you purchase and read the *PMAI® Manual*, which, in addition to providing background and psychometrics for the instrument, offers case studies and other information about archetypes that can enhance your experiences when working with others.

○   ○   ○
## Exercises for Working in Groups

Once everyone has taken the PMAI® assessment, you may wish to set aside a time to discuss the results together. This process can take many forms—everything from an "archetype" party where participants dress up as their dominant archetype to simply getting together to share results with one another. The following exercises and ideas will help you and others understand and apply archetypes in your daily lives.

### Exercise One: Getting to Know You

Many people find that it is fun to share their results with spouses, family members, friends, and co-workers. People report that discussing PMAI® results can deepen the discourse of conversation or provide ways to understand each other. One reader described how his whole family took the PMAI® assessment and shared their results after Thanksgiving dinner. Others speak of how they shared with a support group, work team, or loved one.

Sharing PMAI® results in a group does not need to be an overly serious activity. Begin by explaining what the PMAI® assessment is and what it measures. If anyone shows apprehension about issues of privacy, you should explain that results go directly to each individual, who can share as much or as little as he or she wishes.

Once all group members have taken the PMAI® and have their results, invite them to read privately the description of their highest archetypes. The next step is to share this information with everyone else. This can be done by highlighting sentences and phrases that are most relevant and then reading them aloud. Some people prefer to put the ideas in their own words. When someone is confused about some part of the description—as it does or does not relate to him or her—use the resources of the group to help that person.

A member may wish for specific feedback about how he or she expresses the characteristics of the dominant archetype. If members wish to share at that level, remember that feedback should be constructive and supportive. Most groups who come together to do this activity automatically share in respectful and appropriate ways. However, if there is a potential for some people within the group to play "gotcha" with the instrument results (using it to show others what is wrong with them), it is best to set ground rules at the beginning.

Here are some appropriate ways to share results:

- Listen to each person's comments and make no remarks until the person sharing indicates comments or questions are welcome.

- Ask genuinely curious questions without probing too deeply, unless group members have agreed upon deeper work.

- Provide feedback only when a person asks for it.

- Emphasize the positive–where you see the gifts of the archetype in the person's behavior.

- If a person asks for feedback regarding the negative or shadow side of his or her dominant archetype, offer this feedback carefully and constructively.

Remember that the focus is not to "fix" people in the group or even to solve their problems; it is to help people know themselves and one another better. Sometimes when people use the PMAI® assessment as a tool to better understand and communicate with one another, problems are resolved in the process.

## Exercise Two: Making a Commitment

This exercise is appropriate for couples considering marriage or civil unions, for people considering going into business together, or for any couple or group making a commitment to live, work, or play together. (This can also be a continuation of exercise one.)

1) Each person describes his or her view of how the marriage, civil union, or partnership should ideally work, using archetypal terms to make clear what narrative they are hoping to live out together.

2) Identify points of agreement and disagreement, seeking to determine if there are one or more stories that are shared and thus could be the basis for finding a common story. For example, one couple agreed to live a central Caregiver story, recognizing that their life together was about caring for one another, their children, and other loved ones. Another couple discovered that their bonding was based on a shared sense of adventure (Seeker story). Yet another couple broke up

because the woman was motivated by care and duty (Caregiver) and the man by fun (Jester). He felt she was a wet blanket, and she thought he was irresponsible. Had they discovered a *third story* that they could share, they might have found common grounds to continue their relationship.

Please note, however, that having a common archetypal story is not necessary for a good relationship or partnership. Most of us are informed by many archetypes as we go through our lives, and often couples will not score high on the same archetype. When partners have different archetypes, it is important to understand each other's stories and how they can complement one another. The couple that ended their marriage might have instead recognized how the Jester can lighten the load and keep the Caregiver from taking herself so seriously, and how the Caregiver can provide the balance of purpose and connection to the Jester.

## Exercise Three: Interpersonal Problem Solving

Identifying the archetypal narratives beneath assumptions can be helpful when two or more people are experiencing a conflict. This can be done on your own if you have taken the time to understand how to use archetypes in this way. If you are uncomfortable pursuing this work independently, you may choose to get help from a mediator, negotiator, counselor, or other third party who is knowledgeable about the use of archetypes in conflict resolution.

If you attempt to do this without professional assistance, please remember the following guidelines:

1) Explain what the PMAI® assessment is and what it measures and how it can be taken (see exercise one).

2) Once everyone has the results, create an archetypal story table to record these results. For example, suppose three people are involved in a conflict. Create a table with three columns and five rows (one column for each person and one row for each person's four highest scoring archetypes; if someone has a tied score, list more than one archetype on a line). Here is an example of how the chart should look:

| Heather | Graham | Kate |
|---|---|---|
| Caregiver | Warrior | Creator |
| Ruler | Destroyer | Ruler |
| Creator | Ruler | Magician/Sage |
| Orphan | Orphan | Orphan |

3) Allow each person a reasonable amount of time to tell his or her view of the situation without being interrupted.

4) Allow some time for respectful questions. The task of the other person (or persons) in the conflict is to hear what each speaker is saying.

5) This format should continue until each person involved has told his or her story about the situation.

6) Next, everyone should tell his or her story again in archetypal terms, referencing the descriptors in the book. This emphasizes the archetypal narrative that influences each person's thinking.

7) Maintaining a genuinely respectful and curious manner, people can raise questions based on their observations about the narrative frame of the story being told. For example, "What I'm hearing is Caregiver when you express the belief that if someone is hurting, others should help. Is that what it feels like to you?"

8) Once all the relevant archetypal stories have been identified, reference the summary PMAI® results that you prepared for each person and explore points of archetypal commonality and divergence. Notice if the stories people have chosen correspond to their highest PMAI® scores.

9) Brainstorm how different archetypal stories might be influencing how each person sees the situation: "Oh, I see how we are all feeling Orphaned and all struggling to be in control and in charge in a Ruler way. But Kate and Heather bond around creating new options (Creator), while Graham tells them what is wrong with their ideas (Warrior and Destroyer)."

10) Finally, the people involved should look for other stories that they could use to transcend the conflict. This process can be facilitated by generating multiple stories and agreeing upon one that may offer options for fruitful collaboration. Or those involved can look at their highest PMAI® scores and see if any one archetype is shared. They can then retell the story from that perspective, looking for clues to the source of the conflict as well as discovering seeds for resolution.

In the example, regardless of the kind of conflict involved, the shared Orphan archetype might make everyone feel victimized, abandoned, or betrayed by everyone else. In such a case, it might make sense to look for the causes of conflict within the organization (or relationship) or situation rather than between individuals. This would be a path worth exploring, especially in regard to a work environment or family dilemma.

## Exercise Four: What Stories Are We Living?

This team–building exercise is appropriate for couples, friends, work teams, and other groups that have joint responsibility for a family, organization, company, or other group. In this situation, it is useful to create a chart summarizing the archetypal results for each person in the group. You can list the three or four highest scores for each person, or for a more thorough approach you can list results for each person for all twelve archetypes from the highest to the lowest score.

1) Explain what the PMAI® instrument is and what it measures and how it can be taken (see exercise one).

2) When everyone has the results, create a table with room for each person's name across the top plus twelve rows for each of the archetypes. List each person's archetypes with scores in descending order (if there are ties, let each person make a judgment about which one to list first). For example, if five people are involved, your chart might look like this:

| Dan | Kate | Jennifer | David | Josh |
|---|---|---|---|---|
| Ruler 29 | Ruler 30 | Creator 30 | Ruler 28 | Jester 30 |
| Caregiver 26 | Sage 28 | Magician 29 | Magician 28 | Creator 29 |
| Magician 24 | Innocent 26 | Innocent 29 | Jester 25 | Seeker 29 |
| Seeker 24 | Magician 26 | Destroyer 27 | Warrior 24 | Warrior 27 |
| Orphan 22 | Warrior 23 | Lover 27 | Lover 22 | Sage 26 |
| Warrior 20 | Jester 22 | Ruler 26 | Sage 21 | Magician 25 |
| Lover 19 | Creator 18 | Caregiver 24 | Creator 18 | Caregiver 24 |
| Innocent 16 | Lover 18 | Orphan 23 | Orphan 16 | Innocent 20 |
| Sage 15 | Seeker 16 | Warrior 21 | Caregiver 16 | Lover 18 |
| Jester 13 | Caregiver 15 | Seeker 19 | Orphan 13 | Destroyer 17 |
| Creator 10 | Destroyer 13 | Jester 17 | Destroyer 12 | Ruler 12 |
| Destroyer 8 | Orphan 12 | Sage 16 | Innocent 10 | Orphan 10 |

3) Make this chart available to all involved (on flip–chart paper, in a PowerPoint presentation, or as a handout). Discuss the following:

- *Which archetypal stories are high for all or most of us (24 or higher)?*
- *What does this mean for what we are likely to notice and do?*
- *Which archetypal stories are low for all or most of us (18 or lower)?*
- *What might we fail to notice or do?*
- *Do we need to bring in other people to help us with this, or can we remember to consciously bring in this perspective ourselves? (Or is it not important or relevant to utilize archetypal analysis to deal with the problem at hand?)*

- *What stories are high for some, but not all of us?*

- *How can we be sure to value and hear the perspectives that might be different from those of the majority of the group?*

- *Are there any archetypes that score very low for one person and very high for another? Is one person living out what the other may have deemphasized or repressed? Could this result in miscommunication, annoyance, or tension between these two?*

- *What archetypes are at midrange (18-24) for all or most of the group?*

- *Are we motivated to live these stories? Do they give us juice, or are they old habits and thus deadening or boring?*

- *If the latter, what activities might be dropped, reassigned, or delegated (even outsourced) to others?*

- *Overall, to what degree does the archetypal energy available to this group support our mission and what we are trying to accomplish?*

○　○　○

## Additional Applications

### Spiritual Development

- *Christian Bible study and spiritual enrichment:* Teach the archetypal stories with examples from the life of Jesus to illustrate the highest attainment of Christian life. Assign members to find biblical stories that illustrate their high archetypes. For Catholics, members could also consider archetypal patterns in the lives of saints.

- *Jewish studies of the Hebrew scriptures and traditions:* Find scriptural stories to illustrate the archetypes of the individuals participating in the study group, or assign group members to do so. Consider how different Jewish rituals and holidays promote the ideal of human development in the Jewish tradition.

- *In Buddhism and other meditative traditions:* Identify meditative practices that promote the virtues of each of the twelve archetypes.

- *In any spiritual tradition:* Consider the expression of each archetype within sacred texts, spiritual practices, sacraments, and holidays.

### Study Groups

Whether you are reading novels, learning about history, or discussing politics, you can explore the archetypal stories that are expressed in all these forms.

## Role–playing and Acting

Create ways for participants to act out their dominant archetypes in various styles and modalities. Follow this with acting out of less preferred archetypes. Acting teachers can use method-acting strategies in partnership with workshop leaders, coaches, and psychotherapists to help people find and express archetypes that may be dormant or expressed in their shadow sides.

## Dancing and Movement

A powerful way to learn the archetypes, especially for kinesthetic learners, is to move or dance each of the archetypes in their positive and negative expressions. Dance instructors can also partner with coaches, workshop leaders, and psychotherapists to help individuals expand their archetypal range through movement and dance.

## Other Artistic Expressions

Singers can sing archetypal songs to express and awaken archetypes; artists can paint, weave, or sculpt the archetypal stories. Any artistic form available to a group can be used to help members experience the archetypal stories and share their inner lives with others.

## Social and Political Action

The archetypal stories can provide a neutral element that may depersonalize conflict. When groups are able to see their own archetypal perspective as one of many perspectives, they are better able to open up to recognizing that another group or opposing force may view the situation through a different archetypal lens (rather than as wrong, evil, or impossible to deal with).

## Transition to Retirement

Often people have difficulty making the transition into retirement. Initially, they may simply want to do whatever has been crowded out of their lives thus far (which is why so many people just want to play when they are first retired). However, after a year or so, ennui can sink in. Retired groups or individuals can use archetypal stories to study and understand this new phase of their lives. Using the PMAI® instrument, they can then support one another to leave the tried and true and to experiment with new behaviors. ○

CHAPTER 6

# Ethical Use of the Pearson–Marr
# Archetype Indicator® Assessment

o     o     o

*The PMAI® assessment, as an entry to the understanding of archetypes and
their influence on life journeys, is a powerful tool for personal insight. Like
any tool, if misused it can be ineffective; or, worse, it can divide people and
inhibit growth. It is thus important that the PMAI® assessment be used
with respect: respect for oneself, respect for those who may share their journey with you, and respect for the instrument itself.*

o     o     o

## Respect for the Individual

*Confidentiality.* One's life journey is among the most personal of experiences. To share that exploration with another is both an honor and a sacred
trust. As the person sharing results, only share with people you have reason

to trust. Anyone authorized to support you in this discovery process is required to treat that information with respect and to ensure it is never revealed to anyone else without your permission. This means that a person may not write or talk about your results and that copies of your PMAI® responses, results, and notes must be kept secure and confidential. If you are helping someone else to understand his or her results, maintain the same confidentiality.

*Sensitivity.* These archetypal systems are designed for self-understanding and to facilitate peer communication. PMAI® results should never be used to trump your own or another's felt experience. Even if you fear you or someone else may be exhibiting some resistance or denial in response to the data, ultimately it is the individual who is the best authority on his or her own life. Do not try to tell a person about his or her journey and do not let anyone–even an expert–tell you about yours. The person who has taken the PMAI® instrument should do most of the talking. It is the job, however, of the professional therapist, counselor, or coach to listen carefully and ask questions to foster understanding and to explain anything about the theories in this guidebook that seem confusing. A professional will explain the results and the theory clearly and directly, separating facts (e.g., one's scores on a given archetype) from hypothesis (e.g., how an archetype may be expressed in one's life at this time). The final decisions about your PMAI® results rest with you.

o   o   o

## Respect for the Materials

The PMAI® instrument is copyrighted; the questionnaire, the interpretive materials, and the manual may not be copied or distributed. The official PMAI® instrument has undergone extensive testing and study to prove its reliability and validity (for more details refer to the *PMAI® Manual*). By purchasing complete and official copies of the instrument and support materials, you will be better able to understand your archetypal journey. If you are using the PMAI® assessment with other people, it is *essential* that you understand the theory behind the instrument. You can further your understanding of the PMAI® instrument through reading, course work, or advanced Jungian studies. (See Resources for more information.)

o   o   o

## Respect for the Process

We each live our own story, which is our own sacred myth. The mythic stories that give our lives meaning are larger than we are; we both live the story and are lived by the story. Moreover, each person's journey is unique and truly a mystery. By showing appreciation for the wisdom and purpose of the process of our lives, we can learn to treat ourselves with more respect. When we see that others are also living great universal stories that provide meaning to their lives, we can also respect them, even when we do not agree with them. Most of the time, respecting the process simply requires you to honor the importance of the stories that are being lived and what gifts they provide. However, sometimes it is beneficial for you (and for others) to find the story, the life myth, that may bring out your latent gifts and enthusiasm for life. Even the process of seeking such an empowering life myth reinforces the idea that each of us is here for a purpose. When we live that story, we experience greater success and fulfillment than we have yet known. The process of finding the deeper meaning behind our lives is often awkward and full of missteps and mistakes. When we are able to see this in our own journeys, it is easier to extend compassion and forgiveness to others while also, of course, maintaining boundaries so we are not unduly hurt by them.

Narrative intelligence (the ability to recognize the story that is being lived out by a person or group) helps us and others see what stories we have been scripted to live and the good or harm they can do. While there are many among us who are wounded to the point that we may need professional help to escape a negative story pattern, most healthy people can develop story vigilance as a normal life skill, starting as young as fourth and fifth grades. Teaching people to pay attention to the stories they are living is important work that should be respected in all areas of life—individual and collective. Such work helps us overcome obstacles, avoid conflicts, and live more harmonious and balanced lives. ○

# NOTES

# CHAPTER 7

# Frequently Asked Questions

o   o   o

**Q:** *What is the most desirable profile?*

The most desirable profile is one that reflects the mystery and uniqueness of your psyche. Having said that, for most people, an ideal profile has a few archetypes that are high enough to give form to your journey and some basis for decision making. (If all the archetypes were equally active, it would be difficult to make a decision, as your archetypes would all have different points of view.) It is also desirable to have some access to as many archetypes as possible, or at least to appreciate people who express their perspectives. (The younger you are, however, the fewer archetypes you may have had time to develop.)

**Q:** *Is a certain profile expected at different times of life?*

No, it is fine to express the archetypes in your own way and in your own order. However, certain archetypes are helpful in responding to the predictable challenges of different stages of life, so they may emerge at these times if they have not done so before.

> Childhood: Innocent and Orphan
> Adolescence: Seeker and Lover
> Early Adulthood: Caregiver and Warrior
> Midlife: Creator and Destroyer
> Maturity: Magician and Ruler
> Elder Years: Sage and Jester

**Q:** *My results seem to me to be quite flat. What does that mean?*

It may mean that you are a conservative test taker and you avoided using the 1s and 5s. It may also mean that you are in transition and many archetypes in your psyche are activated, but canceling each other out. Or, finally, it may mean that you responded to the instrument using too long a time period so that you scored high on archetypes both formerly and currently dominant in your life.

**Q:** *How do I tell if my low scores are a problem?*

They are not likely to be a problem unless you are experiencing the following:

- Difficulty in at least one relationship
- A hard time coping with a situation
- A lack of energy or enthusiasm for life

In any of these cases, it may be important to develop one or more dormant or disowned archetypes.

**Q:** *What if I think the results are accurate but I'd rather express different archetypes? Can I change archetypes?*

It is best to trust the logic of your journey. However, your desire to live a different archetypal journey can also be a call to a new episode. In order to move on, consciously work to get the lesson and the gifts of the archetypes that are active now. In the meantime, expose yourself to movies, plays, novels, music, and role models that relate to the archetype you wish to express in a desirable way. Notice the times and places where you express that archetype and experiment with acting the part until it comes naturally to you.

**Q:** *What if I have no scores of 24 or over?*

This likely results from your being a conservative test taker, avoiding 1 and 5 responses. If you have no archetypes in the 24–30 range, your three to four highest scores are your most active archetypes.

**Q:** *How can understanding archetypes help me at work?*

You can use the knowledge of what motivates you to find career direction or fine-tune current roles. Recognizing the archetypes active in others aids you in understanding and communicating with them. As you learn to awaken archetypes, you can also access qualities and attitudes necessary for career advancement and developing or enhancing your leadership abilities.

**Q:** *Can the PMAI® instrument help me relate better with family and friends?*

Yes, in several ways. When you know which archetypes are most active in *your* life, it will be easier to recognize the expression of archetypes in those people significant to you. This information sensitizes you to their journeys and reminds you that the way people behave may be an expression of only *one part of them* (i.e., the energy from *one archetype*). Understanding archetypes can also help you understand when a friend or family member expresses a particular phase of a journey. For example, if you investigate the attributes of the Caregiver, you can see the gifts and the challenges and be better able to recognize these in someone you know. Understanding another person's journey can help your relations with others.

**Q:** *Several well-known authors advocate letting go of all "stories" in order to live fully in the moment. Does this mean I should leave behind these archetypal stories?*

Like many other words, "story" has more than one meaning. Such authors are advocating letting go of the narratives in our heads that remove us from really living or that fill us with fear, worry, or judgment of ourselves or others. Their point is to live fully, rather than getting lost in the fictions–good or bad–we make up about our lives. Generally, they are also advocating a high level of Sage ability to quiet the mind and experience inner peace and love. But archetypal stories do not remove us from experience (unless we are living them in a trance form). Rather, these archetypal stories help us live more fully and authentically, experiencing at a deep level the potential for what it means to be human. If you are living a story in its archetypal dimension, you can be fully in the moment. If and when we live a story in a way that disconnects us from reality, we can use the PMAI® system to "name" the story and put distance between ourselves and the "fiction" with which we are identifying.

# NOTES

# CHAPTER 8

# The Twelve Archetypes

o    o    o

*This chapter provides comprehensive descriptions of the twelve archetypes. Each archetypal description found there begins with a mythic story or folktale to help explain the context of the archetype. Following that are variations on the basic story pattern for that archetype. Each archetype also has descriptions of its imagery, its gifts, and ways it is seen in nature, spirituality, and leadership. This is followed by ways you might experience the archetype when it is active in you, which is typically reflected by high scores for that archetype. Remember that you may express these archetypes in slightly different ways. Refer to chapter 3 for detailed steps in learning how to explore archetypes in your life.*

# The PMAI® Archetypes

INNOCENT          ORPHAN          WARRIOR

CAREGIVER          SEEKER          LOVER

DESTROYER          CREATOR          RULER

MAGICIAN          SAGE          JESTER

**I N N O C E N T**

*Daphne loved to run in the woods on her father's estate. She would spend her days wandering or hunting, her unkempt hair waving in the wind. At times her father, the river god Peneus, despaired because she refused the affections of even the most eligible suitors, choosing to remain unmarried. "Am I to have no grandson?" lamented Peneus. Daphne would throw her arms around her father's neck and implore him to let her run free like the goddess Diana. Peneus would invariably relent and Daphne would bounce happily back to the woods.*

*One day the god Apollo spotted Daphne running through the woods. Immediately he became enchanted and began to race after her. Even though Apollo was a god, he found it hard to catch the fleet Daphne. Apollo implored her to stop, trying to reassure her. "You have nothing to fear. I am no rude shepherd; I am the lord of Delphi!"*

*But Daphne ran all the faster. Still Apollo gained on the frightened Daphne, until she could feel his breath on her neck. Suddenly the trees parted to reveal the bank of her father's river. "Help me, father! Help!" she screamed.*

*As she screamed, she slowed. Her feet seemed suddenly bound to the earth. Her skin hardened, and leaves began to sprout from her arms and hands. Apollo drew up to find, in place of the beautiful and free Daphne, a small laurel tree.*

*Apollo decreed in his sorrow and despair that the laurel would forever become his tree; and the prize for victors in athletics or in song would always be a wreath of laurel. The little tree bowed and swayed in the breeze as if in assent.*

Adapted from *Mythology: Timeless Tales of Gods and Heroes* by Edith Hamilton.

**The archetypal character:** The archetype which is usually first encountered is the Innocent, presenting a childlike naiveté and trust. The Innocent exemplifies a basic trust in others and in the world as a safe place. Thus for Daphne, the world was a playground of woods and fields, and she showed little inclination or even understanding of growing and changing and assuming a different, more responsible role in life.

The Innocent is the archetype of the innocent child who depends upon adults for care and safety. When the Innocent has a setback, he or she responds by trying harder, and by attempting to have more faith and to be more worthy. This strategy is based on a deep-seated belief that such efforts will be rewarded in time. The Innocent is effectively encouraged in children by an environment of love and safety and by protective limits.

Daphne's story can also be read to illustrate the negative potential within the Innocent stance in the world. She protects her innocence, but in doing so loses her full humanity, becoming a tree instead of a woman. How many of us, in avoiding what we see as temptation or loss, close down, becoming less alive? On the positive side, the Innocent offers the potential for trusting life, bringing with that trust, faith, hope, and wonder.

**The archetypal plot:** The Innocent appears in numerous stories and myths. Think of Sam Gamgee in *The Lord of the Rings*; or the little boy in *Life Is Beautiful*. Most often in stories with an Innocent plot, the Innocent either takes the role of the trusting sidekick (Sam), or the plot concerns the transformation of the Innocent into other archetypal roles (review the story of *Little Mouse* in chapter 1), where the movement is from Innocent to Orphan to Caregiver. In such plots, other characters–Orphans in need, Destroyers as oppressors, Lovers as tempters, Jesters as con artists–can undermine the Innocent's faith.

Other stories that primarily concern the Innocent:

- By far the most common story of the Innocent concerns the relationship with a Caregiver (protector) who, like Peneus or the father in *Life Is Beautiful* or Daddy Warbucks in *Little Orphan Annie*, protects the Innocent from losing his or her trusting view of life (either more or less successfully). With the help of a caregiver, the Innocent can be seen negotiating unanticipated minor conflicts that would otherwise be confounding, as in A. A. Milne's *Winnie the Pooh* (Pooh Bear invariably gets a honey jar caught on his nose, or gets caught in a tree hollow and has to be extricated by Christopher Robin time and time again).

- An Innocent is a pure, naive observer for the tragedy and the irony of the world. The reader or viewer is able simultaneously to see events through the eyes of the world and through the contrasting eyes of the Innocent. *Forrest Gump* becomes witness to world events (e.g., Vietnam, Watergate) and personal calamity (e.g., child abuse, hurricane) but maintains his optimistic, unsophisticated (Innocent) perspective.

○ In the tragic form of the story, the naiveté or the denial of the Innocent becomes a tragic flaw. If there is a Caregiver in the story, that person is unable to save the Innocent (or others around him or her) from their fatal naiveté. Classic examples of this are *Billy Budd* by Herman Melville, in which Billy's speech impediment prevents him from defending himself, with tragic consequences. Another example is the character Lenny in John Steinbeck's *Of Mice and Men*.

○ Beautiful and sometimes inspiring narratives that show the Innocent prevailing because of sheer goodness and a commitment to follow the rules and to do things right exemplify another form of the Innocent story. Tiny Tim in Dickens's *A Christmas Carol*, is such a character, as is the little dinosaur in the children's movie, *The Land Before Time*. More adult patterns include any number of stories about women protecting their virtue, and both women and men protecting their beliefs by being true to them, whatever the cost. In stories such as *The Lord of the Rings* or *The Sound of Music*, the protagonist moves from a naive optimism and faith to face the reality of destructive energies within and/or without, while retaining or rediscovering a basic trust in life.

**Imagery:** The imagery of the Innocent archetype can be the beauty of a green meadow, the peacefulness of the hobbits, or a small quaint town. In times of difficulty, innocence is associated with hope. Thus in winter, at the darkest time of the year, virtually all religions have celebrations that include the lighting of candles signifying the triumph of light over darkness. In the same vein, the star of Bethlehem pointing the way to the Christ child or the north star orienting sailors similarly provide a sense of stability and hope.

**Gifts:** The Innocent has incredible optimism and faith that institutions, authorities, or divinities will provide what he or she needs. Such faith is very important to the development in children of basic trust in life. Author Hugh Marr tells how one of his young daughters, upon finishing her shower, would turn off the water, then stick her hand out from behind the shower curtain, secure in the knowledge that, without needing to say or do anything more, a towel would appear and be placed in her hand! There are also adults who just know they will have whatever they need, and often their faith is justified.

**Social support:** Children need adults to protect them so that they can be dependent and innocent. Even in adulthood, we all need the belief that we will have what we need–jobs, food, transportation, health. There is in most every one of us the sense that the government, our employers, and other organizations should take care of us, and that at least most of the people we encounter will be honest and decent. When family, workplace, and societal supports break down, the Innocent in any of us tends to wither, leaving us bereft of basic optimism and faith in life.

**In nature:** Newborns in most species–whether a baby, a puppy, a kitten, or any other animal–are attractive, endearing, and have features that make us want to care for them. This may be nature's way of ensuring that someone will care for new life when it emerges.

**In spirituality:** The youthful Innocent sees God (or some other spiritual figure) as either a stern or benevolent father or parent who punishes people when they are bad and rewards them when they are good. At a more mature level, Innocents can be mystics who experience spirituality in their daily lives and are filled with awe and wonder at the glory of living, even when life is not perfect.

**As leaders:** Innocents are good at being true to and maintaining traditions. They can effectively apply traditional rule-based approaches to leadership. Unexpectedly, their optimism also allows them to apply state of the art leadership approaches, especially when those approaches are recommended by a mentor. The Innocent leader can be good at inspiring people, seeing opportunities, and staying cheerful and upbeat.

> If the Innocent is active in your life (high score),
> you have faith that every cloud has a silver lining.

**At your best** (now or when you fulfill your potential) as an Innocent, you exemplify what a life of faith and simple goodness brings to the world. You have a basic trust in others and in the world as a safe place, you avoid temptation no matter how strong, and you help the world maintain virtue and fairness. You are now (or potentially) able to model hope, optimism, and the awareness that happiness comes from living a simple, wholesome life. Even when circumstances are difficult, you know how to focus on the positive and not allow the negative to control your sense of yourself or of possibilities for the future. You keep hope alive in the most difficult circumstances either by overcoming problems with positive thinking or by reframing them into opportunities.

**You may want to guard** against underestimating difficulties or in being overly confident in your own abilities. You may be blindsided by unforeseen problems, taken advantage of by people you know, or shaken by being forced to see the dark side of life that you would rather avoid. You can also fall prey to people who promise easy answers that fail to work.

**When problems emerge,** you are likely to apply traditional and time-honored strategies; downplay the seriousness of difficulties; and/or seek an expert to figure out what to do, all the while keeping the faith that the problem can be solved. You may also do nothing, hoping that rescue will come. Or, if frightened, you may call for help, experiencing real trust that help will arrive.

**Others may appreciate** the Innocent's wholesome and upbeat approach to life. When under the influence of the Innocent, you may be seen as naive, in need of protection, and not fully capable of pulling your own share of the load. This can lead to frustration, or even resentment, on the part of others who have enough problems without having also to take care of you. The Innocent may be the straight man to others' jokes, not fully understanding the complexity or irony of the situation. Finally, the Innocent archetype may be taken for granted and not recognized for contributions.

**You tend to notice** what is good and trustworthy and meritorious in the world and in yourself. You may be oblivious to dangers that threaten, to how hard life is for others around you, to your own limitations, or to unconscious dependency.

**You want to be seen as** a nice, good, and positive person, and you want to avoid doing anything that might seem unkind, bad, or to be a drag on others.

### Actions or qualities that you may find beneficial:

- Cultivation of the ability to anticipate difficulties.

- Becoming more circumspect before trusting others.

- Gaining a realistic appraisal of your own abilities–neither underestimating nor overestimating.

- Putting less trust in authorities or in simple easy answers.

- Solving as many of your own problems as you can.

- Balancing the Innocent's virtues with those of the Orphan.

**If one of your lowest scores is Innocent,** you may do one or more of the following (check any that apply):

○ Be overly skeptical, cynical, or despairing, seeing no hope in whatever circumstances you are facing.

○ Get annoyed at people who seem wide-eyed and naive or out of touch with reality.

○ Never have experienced a time or place where you were safe enough to let down, be yourself, and trust others.

○ Have been taught, and believe, that it is not acceptable to be too optimistic or trusting.

**ORPHAN**

*Once there was a little girl whose parents were too poor to keep her, so they sent her to live with her grandmother in the country. The little girl shared many happy times with her grandmother, but at last the grandmother became ill and died. The little girl was returned to her parents in the city. The parents sent her out every day to sell matches on the street. When she returned at night, her father would beat her if she had sold too few matches; and often there would be nothing to eat for dinner. The seasons turned and the weather grew quite cold. The wind whipped between the tall buildings and through the city streets. There were few people out, and those who were hurried past to find warmth inside one of the buildings. The little match girl huddled in a doorway, drawing her bare feet up under her as snow swirled and danced. She thought of returning home, but home was not much warmer than the street, and there was not likely to be anything to eat. Finally she thought of striking one of the matches to see if it would give her fleeting warmth. She struggled to hold the match in numb fingers. After dropping several, she managed to light one on the cobblestones. The tiny light flared up, and there, in the flame, she saw the smiling face of her grandmother. Suddenly her grandmother vanished, and only the barren icy street appeared behind her burned finger. Determined now, the little girl struck another match. There again appeared the laughing eyes of her grandmother. Wouldn't it be wondrous, she thought, if I lit all the matches?! And so, lighting another, she set fire to the whole bundle. There appeared her grandmother—not just her face, but her whole body. Her grandmother reached out her arms and gathered the little match girl to her.*

*In the early light of a winter morning they found the tiny frozen body, barefoot and dressed in rags. She clutched a charred bundle of matches. They were surprised to find she had a smile upon her face.*

Adapted from *The Little Match Girl* by Hans Christian Andersen.

One of the Innocent's defenses against recognizing vulnerability is to believe that bad things happen because you were bad. The little match girl shows the Orphan awareness that bad things happen to the *good and bad alike*. Indeed, the Orphan situation is sometimes hard to face squarely because it raises deep existential questions about why Innocents suffer. The tension within this story is built on feeling sympathy for the girl and sadness or anger at the failure of the parents or of the community to properly care for her. The only hope for her comes in death. At least there she is not orphaned, because the figure of the protector grandmother comes to comfort her.

**The archetypal character:** The archetypal character of the Orphan can be a child lacking the support of those who should be there to help (e.g., the hugely popular children's books, *A Series of Unfortunate Events* by Lemony Snicket), but he or she can also be an adult caught in a powerless situation at the mercy of unfortunate events, oppressive people, or a mental or physical health crisis. Such characters may retreat to cynicism and despair, justifying their oppression or taking advantage of others. They may also reach out and ask for help (in the little match girl's case to a figure beyond the grave). The Orphan within you offers the resilience to survive whatever life throws at you. It can also offer you a humble and accepting attitude.

**The archetypal plot:** Orphan plots begin with trauma, betrayal, or victimization, in which a person learns the skills and perspectives that allow him or her to overcome adversity and/or to survive difficulties. Alternatively, the Orphan fails to do so and is defeated.

Other stories with the Orphan as the main character:

- Fatalistic or cynical stories, such as *Slum Dog Millionaire*, in which a person's neediness leads to victimization or, as in the story of *The Little Match Girl*, the indifference of parents and society leaves the match girl defenseless against the cold. The orphan can also be seen in stories where former victims victimize others (*Hotel Rwanda*).

- Stories in which the dispossessed help one another (e.g., *Braveheart, Easy Rider*) even though their efforts may not be successful. As with *The Rime of the Ancient Mariner* or survivors of the Holocaust, people may tell their stories to help make sure such mistakes, injustices, or atrocities do not happen again.

- Narratives that show the triumph of the underdog and in which Orphans succeed because they help one another (*Good Will Hunting, Seabiscuit*). For instance in *Seabiscuit*, the over-the-hill horse trainer understands that you do not give up on people or horses just because they have been roughed up a bit.

- Stories in which Orphans move from facing their own pain to developing empathy for others in need. This change may often be difficult to identify because the

Orphan transforms into Caregiver, Warrior, and perhaps Sage. (Consider Oprah's rise from inauspicious beginnings to being one of the most influential women in the United States or characters like Celie in *The Color Purple*).

**Imagery:** Orphan imagery includes barren landscapes, broken objects, dejected or emaciated people, grainy images in black and white, ordinary (often working-class) people helping one another out, and even the Statue of Liberty as a symbol of refuge for the tired, lonely, and displaced.

**Gifts:** The Orphan balances the Innocent by facing difficulties and disappointments head on, by becoming a survivor. Such survivors do not have to sugarcoat life. While they are hypervigilant to anticipate and head off difficulties, they also have learned through experience that they have the resilience to cope with whatever happens. Because they have had the courage to face their own fears, they can be there for others.

**Social support:** The Orphan dilemma is generally caused or intensified by a lack of family, community, or governmental support. People are left on their own to cope with situations beyond their control. Orphans often need assistance to help them get back on their feet, but this help need not perpetuate long-term dependence. Those living an Orphan story like to feel as if they are not alone in their troubles. Labor unions (Orphan plus Warrior), twelve-step groups, and other groups are examples of successful social support systems that help people live an Orphan story in a positive way. Immigrants often leave their homeland because of poverty or oppression. Whether or not they succeed in their new lives often depends upon whether others assist them in making the transition. Pioneers in the American west helped each other to survive great difficulties by supporting each other (through barn raisings, quilting bees, etc.). Similarly, state sponsored and charitable welfare programs help people get back on their feet when they are down.

**In nature:** As the high level of the Orphan is the discovery of interdependence and its importance to survival, modern environmental science shows us that even the natural world is interdependent. The ecology of any given area is based on species that need one another, thereby creating an ecosystem in which each life form makes its contribution to the whole. In the human body, interdependent organisms such as intestinal bacteria are essential to our survival. They cannot live without us or we without them. In this context, survival of the fittest does not refer to dominance (the way in which the Warrior archetype would see it); rather it means a coexistence between organisms and systems. This is the interdependence characteristic of the mature Orphan.

**In spirituality:** Like the Innocent, Orphans see God (or some other spiritual figure) as a parent figure. When the Orphan is active in our lives, we may initially imagine that our difficulties are punishments from God or that God has abandoned us, a belief that can lead to a complete loss of religious or spiritual faith. At a more mature level, the Orphan lets go of the assumption that God's role is to protect us from the troubles of life, thereby regaining trust in the ability of God, or some other higher power, to provide comfort, healing, renewal, and strength during hard times. In other words, for the mature Orphan, God does not protect us from having difficult times but instead provides the strength to endure and survive them.

**As leaders:** Orphan leaders are generally realistic about what can be accomplished, do not promise what they cannot deliver, and are good at anticipating and addressing problems. If they have dealt with their own pain or wounding, they are generally empathic with people in difficulty but not likely to let them use excuses to get away with not doing what they are supposed to do (thus exhibiting the practice of tough love).

If the Orphan is active in your life (high score),
you assume that it pays to be careful.

**At your best** (now or when you fulfill your potential), you demonstrate the resilience to survive life's tragedies and disappointments; a deep egalitarian belief in the dignity of ordinary people; a hardboiled realism that does not need to sugarcoat life; and a deep empathy for others, especially those in need. You may also make effective use of self-help, twelve-step groups, or friendship networks; and you may band together with others to advocate for those who are weak, hurt, poor, or otherwise in trouble.

**You may want to guard against** the tendency to be fatalistic, cynical, or fearful of trusting again because as an Orphan you have been let down many times. In fact, the worse things get, the less likely you are to trust others and get the help and support you need. Often you hunker down, protect your turf, and let others cope as best they can. As an Orphan, you can excuse your own hurtful actions with reasons such as "everyone does it," "the person deserved it," "it was really the other person's fault," or you can use the bad things that have happened to you as an excuse for inappropriate behavior.

**When problems emerge,** you may have a tendency to feel like "here we go again." This may trigger a sense of despair or, conversely, boost your confidence in your ability to weather hard times. You tend to articulate the problem clearly (bear witness), emphasizing how serious it may become if not addressed, and work (alone or with others) to get the attention of those who can fix it. Recognizing that not all problems can be solved, you also try to help people support one another to cope with intractable issues that will not go away.

**Others may appreciate** your tough-minded realism, your self-deprecating or sometimes cynical humor (like that in Dilbert cartoons), and your resilience. While others may sympathize with the difficulties you have gone through, they may also be put off by what to them seems like chronic whining, complaining, or negativity. Some may try to rescue you while others may identify you as a target for victimization.

**You tend to notice** and anticipate difficulties so that you can head them off, and you often serve as the "squeaky wheel" that brings attention to a problem. You are careful to discern a person's character before placing any trust in them, and you have an acute awareness that whatever can go wrong, will. You may fail to notice opportunities, especially if they come from unexpected sources or in unanticipated ways.

**You want to be seen as** realistic, tough, and resilient, and you want to avoid seeming naive or like a potential patsy or victim.

### Actions or qualities that you may find beneficial:

- Avoidance of settling for too little instead of setting your sights higher and being willing to excel.

- Collaborating with others for self-help or for economic or political advantage.

- Disconnecting responsibility from blame, so that you can take responsibility for your life without blaming yourself or others when things go wrong.

- Learning what part your own behavior might play in your difficulties and making indicated changes.

- Balancing the Orphan's virtues with those of the Innocent.

**If the Orphan is one of your lowest scores,** you may do one or more of the following (check any that apply):

- ○ Lack compassion for people in need.

- ○ Find people who whine or complain insufferable.

- ○ Fail to notice when you are being mistreated or mistreating yourself.

- ○ Have lived such a privileged life that you do not know what it feels like to be neglected, powerless, abandoned, or victimized.

- ○ Have been taught and believe that it is shameful to be or to feel powerless.

# NOTES

**WARRIOR**

*One morning, in the time of the Middle Kingdom, when Yao was emperor of all the land, the Eastern sky grew a beautiful crimson. Soon the sun rose, shining its bright yellow orb over all the people. But then, once again, the sky glowed crimson down near the horizon, and soon a second sun rose over the hilltops. Curious farmers glanced up. Fishermen put aside their nets to shield their eyes and glance in wonder at the eastern sky. Soon looks of wonder turned to consternation, then to horror as a third sun rose, then a fourth, and a fifth until ten suns began to bake the land. Crops began to turn brown and shrivel; the lakes and rivers shrank to trickling creeks. The people fled into houses and under shade trees, trying vainly to escape the searing heat. In desperation, Yao prayed to Taiyang Dijun, god of the east heavens. It was Dijun who kept the giant mulberry tree in whose boughs rested the ten magical ravens, each of which inhabited a sun. The ravens would take turns, and each day one would carry its sun across the sky. Only now all ten suns had arisen at once, and the earth was in danger of roasting.*

*Dijun heard the emperor's prayer and sent his trusted assistant, Yi, the greatest archer of all time. Yi hoped to find a peaceful settlement, but upon seeing the parched earth, he knew he would have to fight. He was taken to a high tower overlooking the heavens. There he fitted an arrow in his bow and launched the missile straight into the last sun to rise. As the light was extinguished, a shower of black feathers rained down from the sun-raven within it. The people emerged from their dwellings and cheered as a second, then a third and fourth sun were extinguished. By the eighth shot the thousands of black drifting feathers had cooled the earth. Yi raised his great weapon a ninth time, then set it aside as the ninth sun exploded into black feathers. He left the tenth westernmost sun to warm the world for all time.*

Adapted from "The Time of the Ten Suns" in *Mythology: The Illustrated Anthology of World Myth and Storytelling*, edited by C. S. Littleton.

While this story focuses on the heroism of the great archer Yi, the story also presents the devastation that can be caused by violent action, no matter how much it may be justified. Note that Yi's action, while saving the world, destroyed the ravens.

Yao sent Yi on many other missions in the years after the archer saved the earth. Yi fought with the wind god that had created torrential storms, with the river god that caused terrible flooding, and with a huge people-devouring giant.

**The archetypal character:** The Warrior archetype is about achieving goals as well as setting and enforcing boundaries. The Warrior archetype often has a code of honor involving a high level of discipline, principle, and, as in this story, heroism. The Warrior enjoys competing and tends to embark on crusades. At worst, they are ruthless, like Attila the Hun, destroying people without regard to their civilization or culture. More evolved Warriors may show greater understanding of their supposed enemies.

The film *Crouching Tiger, Hidden Dragon* is a captivating portrayal of the Warrior in its many guises, demonstrating the incredible skill and courage of the Warrior. In one scene, the master swordsman defeats a woman who has attacked him and then offers to teach her. However, even those most magnanimous Warriors often pay a price. They are typically stoic and thus deficient in the ability to be intimate and vulnerable, even with the people they love.

**The archetypal plot:** Warrior stories include almost all variations of the war story, accounts of competitive sports or business transactions where the alternatives are winning or losing. The typical plots include a courageous figure who fights to save the underdog, to rescue the damsel in distress, or to overcome a major obstacle (e.g., *Spider Man*; *Harry Potter*; *Saving Private Ryan*; *Rocky*; or any story about how the home team wins, a candidate gets elected, or success is achieved after a long struggle). Thus, the major foils in the story are often the Innocent or Orphan in need of rescue, and the villain (who may be another Warrior, a Destroyer, or occasionally a Caregiver) is seen as emasculating or disempowering the strong (e.g., Nurse Ratchet in Ken Kesey's *One Flew Over the Cuckoo's Nest*). Responding with the Warrior archetype when another archetype is more appropriate tends to lock others in the complementary roles of victim and villain. In fact, Warriors tend toward dualistic thinking, with their attachment to being heroes transforming anyone who disagrees with them into villains.

Other stories that primarily concern the Warrior:

- Stories of courageous and effective action, as with many of John Wayne's characters, or with superheroes such as Superman or Wonder Woman.

- Stories that show the process by which a person develops Warrior courage and determination (Henry Fleming in *The Red Badge of Courage*; Celie in *The Color Purple*; or Yu Shu Lien in *Crouching Tiger, Hidden Dragon*).

- Stories where a heroic person stays true to his or her own vision, even when facing death (as with Joan of Arc).

- Stories where the Warrior fails in the quest, often because of some tragic and unrecognized personal shortcoming. (The story of Achilles in *The Iliad*–invulnerable except in his heel–is the classic example.) The villainous warrior (Darth Vader in *Star Wars*) has his goals corrupted to the extent that power and control become his only ideals.

- Stories of revenge where the hero warrior takes on a mission of payback for past grievances (Uma Thurman's character in the *Kill Bill* series avenges the murder of her husband) or advocacy where a hero takes on the powers that be for a just cause (*Silkwood*)

- Stories where a hero, such as Luke Skywalker in *Star Wars*, starts out with traditional ideas about the enemy only to gain sympathy for the enemy's plight, as Skywalker does when he recognizes that Darth Vader is his father.

- Stories in which the Warrior defeats the enemy within, becoming a spiritual Warrior who overcomes his or her own inadequacies and has the strength of character to seek out nonviolent ways to overcome oppression (Gandhi, Martin Luther King, Aung San Suu Kyi).

**Imagery:** Warrior imagery is bold, dynamic, and often mechanistic, giving a sense of strength, directionality, and focus. It may include big buildings, weapons, or sports arenas, and people moving quickly, with defined, even sharp gestures, with energy directed toward a goal.

**Gifts:** The gifts of this archetype include perseverance in the face of obstacles, the ability to set and defend boundaries, the courage to stand up for yourself and your ideals, the toughness to fight to win, persevering over great odds. The Warrior archetype offers the strength and discipline to achieve goals and to protect personal boundaries.

**Social support:** The Warrior benefits from opportunities to compete in school, in athletics, in business, and in debating ideas. Unless their training is rigorous about following rules and living up to ethical standards, Warriors may be so intent on winning that they are capable of taking unethical action to prevail. For this reason, Warriors thrive when they are trained by teachers, coaches, bosses, or others who model a combination of strength and integrity and who hold them to a high standard. Indeed, Warriors need to be pushed to give their best effort and appreciate not being let off the hook (e.g., in boot camp). For this reason, they may not like the idea of the social safety net because they fear it will encourage people to slack off and be dependent on others.

**In nature:** The Warrior exists in the hunt where one animal pursues, kills, and eats another. The Warrior spirit is also seen in many mammals where the young males or females fight, sometimes to the death, to be head of the herd. The Warrior energy is evident in the competition built into nature: survival of the fittest.

**In spirituality:** Warrior spirituality focuses on doing things correctly, showing discipline, personal responsibility, and often some degree of asceticism. It is prone to holy wars, seeing God or another higher power as the ultimate general, ordering the troops to defeat the enemy without and the sin within. At its highest level, the spiritual Warrior gains the self-control to do whatever he or she believes is the right action, either because it is their job or because it is God's will. In such cases, even violent action (as in a war believed to be just) is motivated by a higher calling to serve God and humankind, even if it means sacrificing one's own life for the greater good.

**As leaders:** Warrior leaders excel at goal setting and implementation, motivating teams to give their best efforts, building winning teams, and constantly critiquing efforts to improve performance. They generally do not put up with slackers or whiners, expecting people to get it together and do what needs to be done. If they believe strongly in something, they will give it all they have, even (as in war) their own lives.

If the Warrior is active in your life (high score),
you assume that the tough prevail.

**At your best** (now or when you fulfill your potential), you model or try to show what it means to have real courage and determination, the kind that allows a hero to face the most fierce antagonist or challenge with skill and determination. You also may have, or desire to have, the fortitude to stand up for your ideals, yourself, or others and do whatever it takes to succeed, regardless of how scared or tired you may be. You have a code of honor that requires a high level of discipline and a strong sense of pride, so that you feel humiliated if you lose or show cowardice. You enjoy competing and/or spearheading a crusade. You are at your best when you are on a mission.

**You may want to guard against** the Warrior's tendency to view the world in terms of black and white, avoiding gray areas and perceiving those who have different ways or opinions as wrong or bad. Warriors can get locked in contests or even wars that leave devastation in their wake. When your commitment to doing what it takes gets out of control, you may need to guard against burnout. You may find it difficult to care for yourself, perhaps because you cannot face the fact that you have vulnerabilities, needs, and frailties. You might do well to remember that even great Warriors need some rest and relaxation.

**When problems emerge,** you tend to do whatever you have been doing but longer and harder. You face problems directly and defend your boundaries and those of others. You also tend to identify enemies or antagonists that you see as causing the problems, and you set out to defeat them.

**Others may appreciate** your strength, decisiveness, and capacity to win. In fact, you embody a cultural ideal, which traditionally has been associated with men; however, the concept of women as Warriors (Xena Warrior Princess) can be equally appreciated. Friends and loved ones may worry that you will burn yourself out and that you are so stoic that you fail to recognize or express your feelings. To some people, you may seem so aggressive or ruthless that you scare them. Nevertheless, others will try to enlist you to deal with difficult situations and to rescue them when they are in trouble.

**You tend to notice** injustice, challenges, and antagonists, and you develop strategies to overcome them in order to achieve your goals. In people, you focus on how tough or skilled people are, and in addition you note any weaknesses that have to be shaped up so they do not let you down. In framing solutions, you tend to be attracted to either/or scenarios. You may be unable to recognize the talents and contributions that can be made by people who in your eyes seem weak or inferior.

You want to be seen as tough, competent, and in control; you want to avoid seeming weak, vulnerable, or needy.

**Activities or qualities that you may find beneficial:**

- Choosing battles wisely, realizing that not every situation needs to be either combative or competitive.

- Seeking enough rest and relaxation to stay healthy and refreshed, taking time to recognize and express your vulnerabilities.

- Working to see the point of view of others, even your competitors or adversaries.

- Hanging back so that others might show what they can do for themselves (because not everyone always needs rescuing).

- Avoiding either/or thinking and instead seeking out win/win solutions.

- Balancing the virtues of the Warrior with those of the Caregiver.

**If the Warrior is one of your lowest scores,** you may do one or more of the following (check any that apply):

○ Get run over by others who see you as weak.

○ Have difficulty setting limits or saying "no."

○ Avoid competitive situations.

○ Have difficulty being planful and self-disciplined.

○ Dislike people who seem pushy, aggressive, or even bullying.

○ Let others push you around and then ruminate on how bad they are.

○ Never have been in a situation where you needed to fight for yourself or others.

○ Been taught to believe that you should never get angry, lash out, or do anything that disadvantages someone else.

## CAREGIVER

*Demeter, goddess of the grain, brought agriculture to Greece. She enjoyed making the crops grow so the people would be nourished and could prosper—giving to them out of pure generosity without any need to be rewarded for doing so. Demeter loved her sweet daughter Kore, who was beautiful but not quite old enough to marry. But without warning Kore was abducted to the underworld by the god Hades, who had fallen in love with her. At first Demeter did not know where Kore was, so she traveled the world in distress and despair looking for her. She was befriended by Hecate, goddess of the crossroads, who took her to see the sun god, Apollo (who had looked down and seen what happened). Apollo explained that Hades had his brother Zeus's permission to abduct Kore. Now Demeter was furious. Zeus was not just the primary god, he was also Kore's father. He should have been looking out for Kore, and more than that, he should have consulted with Demeter and Kore about what they wanted. Demeter sent emissaries pleading to get her daughter back, but none of the gods would help her.*

*In the first recorded sit-down strike, Demeter sat down and refused to make the grain grow. People began to starve. Finally, Zeus gave in because he realized, if he did not do so, there would be no one left to worship him. Kore—who came to be known as Persephone, queen of the underworld—returned to the earth and immediately not only did crops begin to grow again, but flowers sprang up beneath her feet. However, Persephone told her mother that she ate three pomegranate seeds while in the underworld, so she must return there for three months of the year. This is why we have winter; every year during the time that Demeter grieves the loss of her daughter, the crops do not grow. Kore, however, seemed happy enough in both places, as statues show her smiling both with her mother and with her husband, Hades.*

Traditional Greek myth adapted from *Mythology: The Illustrated Anthology of World Myth and Storytelling*, edited by C. S. Littleton, and *Mythology: Timeless Tales of Gods and Heroes* by Edith Hamilton.

This famous story shows the typical Caregiver dilemma. Demeter begins giving out of her own sense of fullness and generosity, only pulling back and setting boundaries when she feels taken for granted by those who benefit from what she has done. A subtext suggests, moreover, that her love for her daughter may also be a bit controlling, as Demeter has difficulty letting her grow up and have her own life. A further segment of the story tells us that Demeter and Persephone founded the Eleusian mysteries that first taught girls, and then adult women and men, about the laws of agriculture as well as sexuality, birth, maturation, and death.

**The archetypal character:** Caregivers are typically kind people, who gain satisfaction from caring for others. At best, they inspire the world with their compassion (Princess Diana, Mother Theresa, or those who searched the wreckage for survivors after the World Trade Center terrorist attack). Caregivers believe in the golden rule but are often better at "doing unto others," than letting others "do unto them." Because their lives are so linked to their children and others they help, however, they may unconsciously seek to keep them dependent in order to keep them close. At worst, they can become codependent, diverting themselves from their own issues by being overly involved with trying to save others.

The Caregiver within you offers the potential to be genuinely caring and altruistic as well as a great humanitarian.

**The archetypal plot:** In the classic Caregiver story, a kind and giving person demonstrates generosity by helping others in ways that make a real difference (examples include the movie *It's a Wonderful Life*, the children's story *The Giving Tree*, and the book *All Things Great & Small*). Others show their gratitude by giving back; or the Caregiver learns to balance care for others with care for oneself.

Other characters essential to the Caregiver plot are the Innocent and Orphan, who need care, nurturing, and/or protection. Generally there is also an antagonist who causes problems either by neglecting or harming the person in need or who stands in the way of allowing the Caregiver to provide aid (although in some cases, as in the movie *Steel Magnolias*, the antagonist is an illness not a person).

Other stories that primarily concern the Caregiver:

- Stories that extol the virtues of giving (*The Giving Tree, All Things Great and Small*).

- Devouring mothers or controlling fathers who, because of their own anxiety, risk ruining the lives of their children and of others because they cannot let them go (Luke Skywalker's uncle in *Star Wars*).

- The Caregiver learning to establish boundaries and determine when to let others solve their own problems (Demeter refusing to make the crops grow until her demands are met.)

- A caregiving figure that intervenes when others are neglected (Mary Poppins) and sets things straight. At a spiritual level, this may be someone willing to sacrifice his or her life for others (the lion in the movie *The Chronicles of Narnia: The Lion, the Witch, and the Wardrobe*, based on the *Chronicles of Narnia* series by C. S. Lewis).

**Imagery:** Caregiver imagery includes the cornucopia; images of abundance; harvest; and smiling, kind-looking people bending toward others in a benevolent way. Images of home and family, a fire in the hearth, soft colors, and rounded shapes are also symbolic of the Caregiver.

**Gifts:** Caregivers find satisfaction caring for and even sacrificing for others, gaining the gifts of altruism, compassion, and nurturance. At their best, they are saint-like in their generosity.

**Social support:** In a highly competitive economy, people are most often rewarded for achievement, rather than care and concern for others. Yet societies prosper when they value the gifts of the Caregiver, which can be exemplified through the efforts of parents caring for children, adults caring for aged parents, friends and neighbors helping one another. In a society that values the gifts of the Caregiver, individuals can be rewarded for providing that role. The Caregiver archetype is one that is often honored by religious, governmental, and educational institutions that encourage altruism.

**In nature:** Birds sit on their nests to keep their eggs warm and feed the baby chicks (*March of the Penguins*). Mammals suckle their young and often care for one another. Dogs care for people. Caregiving is clearly associated with species survival, and this impulse is considered one factor that increased the survival ability of homo sapiens. The Caregiver archetype is exemplified in the body's chemical response to caregiving activities: endorphins are released when we do good deeds for others, and in women, particularly, the fight or flight response is replaced with a tendency to tend and befriend.

**In spirituality:** For Caregivers spirituality is about altruism and transcending the smaller self through focusing on the needs of others. Generally this involves donating money; showing love for neighbors; befriending the lonely; and helping the sick, the poor, the elderly, and those in trouble. The Caregiver archetype expresses love for God (or recognition of a greater power) through fidelity to the spiritual path and sacrifice for the greater good.

**As leaders:** Leaders who express the Caregiver archetype have a wonderful ability to take care of those they lead–whether family members, employees, constituents, or community members. They also have a natural ability to provide customer or client services. Those who express this archetype partner well with other individuals and groups because they are trusted. However, such leaders may also allow people with a good "sob" story to get away with underperforming. Caregiver leaders that have a wider global perspective are good at organizing people in charitable, humanitarian, and philanthropic efforts.

> If the Caregiver is active in your life, you
> assume you have a responsibility to help others.

**At your best** (now or when you fulfill your potential), you may demonstrate a saintly nature, full of love and caring for your fellow creatures. You model altruism both in material ways and in seeing others with kind, compassionate, and forgiving eyes. You make the world a safer and gentler place for everyone. In most of your relationships, you act like a caring parent who creates nurturing environments where people can heal or grow.

**You may want to guard against** the Caregiver's tendency to use control and manipulation to get people to do what you think is best for them. Caregivers may be uncomfortable asserting their needs directly, making it easier to use guilt or other means to get their way. In their desire to help, they martyr themselves, undermine their health, and, in modeling this behavior, implicitly pressure others to burn themselves out as well. If they are not careful, they also enable others' weaknesses, reinforcing rather than reducing their dependency.

**When problems emerge,** your tendency is to notice who is hurting and try to do whatever you can to help them, perhaps even without thought to what it will take to do so. You are likely to provide emotional sustenance and comfort, to guide and teach, to perform maintenance tasks that allow a system to operate (cleaning, repairing, editing, decorating, etc.), and to build a sense of community characterized by nurturing relationships.

**Others may appreciate** your kindness and generosity, take advantage of you, or deride you as controlling and codependent.

**You tend to notice** problems concerned with the physical and emotional side of life: poverty, ill health, and the ways people hurt one another. You immediately take action to help people in need. You also focus on resources and strategies for helping, being open to a wide field of possibilities for aid and comfort. Everything else, including your own health and well-being, may escape notice, except in exhaustion. At that time what beckons is anything that revives energy (such as a good meal or a talk with a close friend).

You want to be seen as generous and caring, and you want to avoid doing anything to seem selfish, self-aggrandizing, or egotistical.

Actions or qualities that you may find beneficial:

- Making sure your own physical and emotional needs are met, showering the same quality of care on yourself that you habitually show to others.

- Expecting others to do everything they can for themselves, thus avoiding the unconscious habit of enabling others' weaknesses and fostering dependency.

- Learning to have good boundaries, saying "no," protecting your time and priorities.

- Letting others give to you and appreciating their efforts on your behalf.

- Balancing the virtues of the Caregiver with those of the Warrior.

**If Caregiver is one of your lowest scores**, you may do one or more of the following (check any that apply):

○ Have a hard time taking care of anyone else and be seen by others as selfish.

○ Feel irritated at people who are always trying to help you or others.

○ Find that it is hard for you to sympathize with people's problems.

○ Have never been in a position where you were expected to help another person.

○ Have been cautioned about the dangers of being codependent.

○ Determined you did not want to be devalued like some Caregivers you have known.

# NOTES

**S E E K E R**

*A Spanish shepherd, Santiago, awakening from his sleep in an old abandoned church-yard, seeks out a fortune-teller to tell him what the dream means that he keeps having night after night. He tells her that in the dream a child comes to him and tells him of a treasure buried at the foot of the Pyramids. The fortune-teller encourages him to embark on a quest to find this treasure and he does. However, there are many challenges on this pilgrimage. He sells everything he has, and books passage for Tangiers, Africa, where a guide he engages steals all his money. Fortunately, he finds work in a crystal shop, where he discovers that he has a gift for selling, greatly enhancing his boss's business. Paid fairly for his great contribution, he joins a caravan to cross the desert, which is no mean feat, as warring bands are fighting all around him. On this journey, he meets a teacher—an alchemist—from whom he learns and then practices all the skills to thrive in the desert and to escape captivity.*

*Finally, he arrives at the Pyramids and starts digging. Three men appear, beat him up, take his money, and laugh at him when he explains to them why he is there. One of the men tells of a dream of buried treasure in an abandoned churchyard in Spain, saying he would not be stupid enough, just because of a dream, to travel there. The shepherd imme-diately realizes where the gold is, travels home, and finds it, just where treasure always is: in one's own backyard (for him, the abandoned churchyard) or in oneself.*

*A journey is always necessary to discover who we are and what we can do—way beyond what we initially thought possible—but the treasure is, therefore, always within.*

Condensed from *The Alchemist* by Paulo Coelho.

This story illustrates the essential tension within the Seeker's story between looking outward for fulfillment and the need to find purpose and identity within. This tension is often resolved when we discover who we are through our experiences in the outer world and by living out adventures exploring the potential within the world around us.

**The archetypal character:** The Seeker is active in a person on a quest, pilgrimage, or adventure that takes place in order to satisfy an inner hunger or yearning. Often there is an inner tension between the drive to fit in and the deeper drive to be true to oneself. While the Seeker fears the loneliness that can result from individuality, he or she is more afraid of the emptiness of not ever knowing or expressing one's true self.

The Seeker archetype provides the energy for finding one's uniqueness and for doing whatever it takes to be true to oneself through a sense of adventure and exploration.

**The archetypal plot:** The Seeker leaves a confining or boring situation and takes some kind of inner or outer journey (Harry Potter leaving the restrictive and abusive confines of his aunt and uncle's house for Hogwarts, or the children leaving the stern and formal mansion through the wardrobe in *The Lion, the Witch, and the Wardrobe*). After many adventures, Seekers either find what they seek (generally some place where they can be true to themselves and fit in) or fail to do so (tragic form). Sometimes the Seeker is forced into a journey (Dorothy in *The Wizard of Oz*) or sets out voluntarily (Johnny Appleseed). Typically, when a person acts out the Seeker plot, others may take the roles of sidekicks on the journey or as oppressors prohibiting the journey.

Other stories that primarily concern the Seeker:

- Stories about figures who perpetually seek an elusive "something" just beyond their grasp or who simply enjoy the journey. This is the basic structure of science fiction, as well as quests, pilgrimages, and travelogues (John Steinbeck's *Travels with Charley*, William Least Heat Moon's *Blue Highways*, Mark Twain's *The Adventures of Huckleberry Finn*).

- Coming of age stories, where a young person leaves home and goes on a journey that provides the challenges needed to grow up (Huckleberry Finn). In the process, Seekers learn to question what they have been previously taught, develop their own opinions, and make their own choices. Sometimes they remain alienated from their roots, and other times not.

- Tragic stories of people forever alienated because they cannot be authentic and still fit in–anywhere–or who isolate themselves out of a chronic fear of conforming (Howard Hughes as portrayed in *The Aviator*).

- A catastrophic event happens and the hero must leave home, and then seeks a new home–a place where it is possible to be authentic and fit in (exemplified in

*The Wizard of Oz* or in the Exodus story from the Bible). If the hero returns home, that place seems different because the hero has transformed. For instance, at the end of the story, Kansas is different for Dorothy because, having taken her journey, *she* is different.

- Stories of ambition—exploring capabilities by scaling a mountain, sailing around the world, or seeing how far one can go in climbing the ladder of success (e.g., *Into Thin Air*).

- Stories about the call to the quest. For example, the search for the Holy Grail in the King Arthur legends invites each knight to enter the forest. As the knights follow their own paths, some succeed in finding not only their vocations but the deeper spiritual meaning of their lives, while others wander without success.

**Imagery:** Seeker imagery includes the horizon receding ahead, mountain ranges and other vertical images (ladders), and people looking off into the distance or walking away from the viewer.

**Gifts:** The gifts of the Seeker include a solid sense of independent identity, great memories of an adventurous life, and a sense of adventure and curiosity.

**Social support:** So many times people are punished or exiled for being true to themselves. Seekers need to have the room to explore and focus on themselves and what is possible for them, without others acting abandoned or aggrieved. Parents often expect their children to make the choices that the parents think are best. Young people (especially in the formative years of finding themselves) need to know they are loved and valued for who they really are, and they need support to find and value their gifts.

**In nature:** Every snowflake, every insect, every star, every ocean has a unique journey to follow, a unique task to perform. Every species has a purpose and the desire to fulfill its destiny (as an acorn "seeks" to become an oak tree). The ultimate gift of the Seeker journey is to find one's own destiny and to live it.

**In spirituality:** The Seeker helps people find their "inner light" or the part of them that is divine and that can be their inner guide. This journey may be done with others who share a belief in the importance of finding the divine within or, more often, as a solitary spiritual quest to find one's own answers.

**As leaders,** Seekers are independent and individualistic, gung ho, adventurous, and willing to try new ideas. Because they embody a "don't fence me in" attitude themselves, they allow others great autonomy—as long as results are attained. While some people quake in fear at today's rate of change, Seekers love it, preferring the new to the tried and true. Because of this, they are often pioneers and entrepreneurs, always scanning the environment for new ideas, new tools, and new talent.

........................................................

If the Seeker is active in your life, the grass
always looks greener somewhere else.

........................................................

**At your best** (now or when you fulfill your potential), you are wonderfully adventurous, independent, and self-sufficient. You refuse to live a cookie-cutter life, always seeking out new experiences, testing the limits of what is possible. Avoiding conformity, you search for your true identity and struggle to fulfill your true potential. Ambitious by nature, but not conventional, you may aspire to climb a mountain or the ladder of success, or to achieve enlightenment. Whatever your goals, you seek to improve yourself, every day becoming more your true self.

**You may want to** guard against the Seeker's tendency to be a perpetual Peter Pan, who won't grow up and accept adult responsibilities and commitments. Seekers may also lose those they love because of others feeling abandoned by their need for independence and freedom. In avoiding conformity, Seekers can go too far, becoming not just eccentric but misfits. In fact, some could end up lonely and alone, being so oppositional that they alienate others who try to get close.

**When problems emerge,** your tendency is to take off and leave them behind. However, you are also good at looking everywhere you can to find new ideas or approaches that might work, and thus you can serve as a scout or pioneer, bringing back solutions from the outer edges of a field or of society that others might not know or trust.

**Others may appreciate** your adventurousness, integrity, and refusal to conform to social expectations. However, they can also experience you as abandoning, alienated and alienating, and lacking loyalty and team spirit.

**You tend to notice** the new and exotic, keeping your eyes constantly on the horizon. You are also keenly aware of the aspects of your present life that are unsatisfactory, limiting, or alienating, and you use them as motivation for your next journey. In groups, you focus on the ways you are different, and you notice how others compromise to belong. You may miss the everyday wonders right at your feet and the way others accept you for yourself, however idiosyncratic you may be.

**You want to be seen as** unique and special, so you avoid doing anything that might make you appear conformist or ordinary.

Actions or qualities that you may find beneficial:

- Keeping in touch with those you truly value

- Noticing ordinary pleasures right here, right now; finding joy in the journey itself, not its end

- Testing out the potential for being true to yourself and your community

- Remembering that you are still an individual, even if you are not calling attention to how you differ from the group

- Balancing the virtues of the Seeker with those of the Lover

**If the Seeker is one of your lowest scores**, you may do one or more of the following (check any that apply):

- ○ Find yourself compromising what you want and believe in order to fit in.

- ○ Avoid traveling or experiencing new things.

- ○ Avoid thinking about yourself and what you want and believe.

- ○ Get annoyed at people who always seem to have to be different.

- ○ Have never had the opportunity to focus on who you are or what you want, or

- ○ Have been told it is selfish or bad to focus on yourself.

# NOTES

# LOVER

*Ceyx was of noble birth; he was the son of the Morning Star, the light that heralds the coming of the day. His wife, Alcyon, was likewise of noble lineage, for she was the daughter of the god of the wind. The two are said to have been devoted to each other and ruled the kingdom of Thessaly with a benevolence that sprang from their love. The king and queen were rarely apart, so much did they enjoy each other's company.*

*But one day Ceyx confessed to his wife that he was troubled and wished to consult the oracle far across the sea. Alcyon begged to accompany him, but Ceyx would not put his beloved wife in peril. Alcyon watched tearfully until the ship was far out at sea. That very night hurricane force winds whipped the seas into mountainous waves and the rain pelted in sheets. Ceyx thought only of Alcyon; indeed, it is said that her name was upon his lips when the little ship listed and sank beneath the dark turbulent waters.*

*Alcyon wove a beautiful robe for the king's return, and prayed to the goddess Juno. Juno, moved by her prayer, sent her a dream. In the dream Ceyx told her that it was her name he had uttered at the last. Alcyon awoke herself crying "wait for me!" As the dawn lightened the eastern sky, she ran to the headland where she had watched Ceyx's ship so long ago. There, on the tide, she saw something floating. As the waves washed it nearer to the shore, she recognized in horror the body of her dear husband. She leaped from the pinnacle toward the water, but instead of plunging beneath, she floated just above the surface. Feathers now covered her body, and her arms had become wings. The body of Ceyx, too, rose from the water buoyed by air—for he, too, had become a seabird.*

*And when you are near the sea, you can still see a pair of birds skimming over the waves. No matter how stormy the seas become, there are always seven days in a row of calm. It is then that the seabirds make their nest upon the waters. These are, indeed, what we call (h)alcyon days.*

Adapted from "Eight Brief Tales of Lovers" in *Mythology: Timeless Tales of Gods and Heroes* by Edith Hamilton.

**The archetypal character:** The most well-known Lover archetype is the hero or heroine of a love story, but anyone who loves anyone or anything deeply can be a Lover. Generally, Lovers are attractive and charismatic, pulling people towards them by the force of their personalities. There is an inner tension within the Lover between the desire to experience many loves (Don Juan) and the desire to commit to one person. There is also within the Lover archetype a connection between love and death, as we see in the story above. The Lover has a desire to merge with the other (a friend, a group, an activity, or even the divine), but to experience that union fully is to lose the self and one's sense of separate being. The challenge for the Lover in everyday life is to maintain commitment while still keeping a separate sense of self. Without that, those who express the Lover archetype may lose themselves in relationships and end up resenting their loss of individuality. Yet, love stories that end with the lovers choosing death over being apart reflect the belief that great loves may transcend death.

The Lover energy within offers you the chance to develop your attractiveness, to attract people who will love you, to choose to do what you love, and to become a loving person.

**The archetypal plot:** We know the Lover story most directly through romance novels and comedies, as well as the great love stories in literature, movies, opera, and art. The basic plot usually involves two people who are attracted to one another, but obstacles keep them apart—often miscommunications. In the course of the story, the two people overcome the obstacles, fall in love, and commit to one another (the classic happy ending as in *Sleepless in Seattle*). Alternately, they may never get together, break up, or even die (*Romeo and Juliet*).

Other stories with the Lover as the main character:

- Stories about great lovers of life (*Zorba the Greek* or *Shirley Valentine*), or of how people find themselves by finding what they love to do (work, play) and where they most like to be.

- Love 'em and leave 'em stories of sexual seduction told from the seducer's point of view (possibly a comedy) or from the point of view of the person who has been seduced and abandoned (usually tragedies).

- Stories such as O. Henry's *The Gift of the Magi*, which recount the sacrifices people make when they are truly committed to one another; or, as in the myth of Alcyon and Ceyx, how commitment survives challenges (in this case even beyond the grave).

- Stories of committed friendship or bonding between groups and work teams that really love one another.

○ Stories of spiritual love where the goal is union with the divine. St. Francis of Assisi, although monastic, was a great Lover, as was the great Sufi poet and mystic, Rumi.

**Imagery:** Lover images include hearts, flowers, the moon in the night sky, sand dunes, beaches (such as in the movie *From Here to Eternity* when the lovers kiss in the surf), soft colors, circular and curving shapes, and other natural or sensuous objects.

**Gifts:** The gifts of the Lover are intimacy, sensuality, closeness, and most of all a heightened capacity for love of others, of beauty, and of life.

**Social support:** The Lover archetype is threatened on the one hand by societies that are too puritanical or on the other hand by societies where sexual behavior is portrayed or approached casually or recreationally. The Lover archetype is enhanced by helping people understand the different kinds of love they experience–romantic, familial, friendship, love of work, love of country–and encouraging them to show their love openly and in appropriate ways. Sometimes the expression of love can be considered taboo, as in the workplace or public life. Full expression of the positive nature of the Lover archetype allows people to share love, passion, and connections in all areas of life, from intimate relationships to support for causes, places, and ideas.

**In nature:** The concept of union, sexual or otherwise, is a primary force of the Lover archetype. As expressed in nature, this force involves everything from the non-emotional union of microscopic creatures to the deep commitment that human beings make to each other. Even animals express the Lover archetype. Geese, for instance, mate for life; and even after the death of a mate, some songbirds continue the mate's song, integrating it with their own. Human sexuality transcends that of the animal world in moving the natural union of partners beyond a purely biological function to a meaningful relationship spanning long periods of time. According to astrologer and theologian Brian Swimme (*The Universe Is a Green Dragon: A Cosmic Creation Story*), the Lover archetype can even be expressed in the universe: gravity acts as the cosmic allurement (love) for the orbits of stars, planets, and galaxies, which are defined by their mutual attraction to other objects.

**In spirituality:** All the great religions of the world tell us to love one another, and for most, marriage is a central sacrament. The ability to love your fellow creatures is generally regarded as a sign of spiritual attainment. Learning to love more every day–and having gratitude for everything you love–is the Lover's spiritual path.

**As leaders,** Lovers have great passion and enthusiasm. As a result they generate similar passion in others, so that people willingly work very hard and gain satisfaction from doing so. They also have a gift for helping people on teams bond, so that they are friends as well as co-workers. If they have developed their emotional intelligence, people who express the Lover archetype are wonderful at providing an atmosphere where people can discuss conflict honestly but still care for one another.

If the Lover is active in your life, you
believe that love is the answer.

**At your best** (now or when you fulfill your potential) you are sensuous, alive, vital, and full of love for others and for life. You would always prefer to be passionately in love with someone who returns your affections, but you also fall in love with cherished activities, the vocation that is your calling, children, pets, and beautiful surroundings and material possessions. You may well have a knack for helping individuals and groups appreciate one another and hence become very close and intimate with others. Your love differs from that of the Caregiver because you see others as peers, not people in need of help. When you shower your attentions on people, they feel the magic of your charisma. A romantic and bliss seeker, you create experiences that help people know what it is like to experience at least a touch of the ecstatic; or, failing that, a time that feels really special.

**You may want to guard against** being promiscuous, becoming infatuated with hurtful people, or injuring others by dropping them when your infatuation cools. Or, in your enthusiasm, you may play favorites and exclude or hurt people. You can also feel empty when not loving or being loved. Some people may see you as vain, cliquish, or shallow, or even as a drama queen or king.

When problems emerge, you look to see how relationships have broken down between individuals or groups. Then you tend to heal this breach through communication, helping people to share what is bothering them and to restore love, friendship, or harmony. You help others (or yourself) become more beautiful (in body, clothes, mind, heart, and/or soul). You may believe that most problems of life can be solved if people, even from diverse cultures and with different ideas, open their hearts and love one another.

**Others may appreciate** your loving nature, your passion and friendliness, and your intensity. Some people may even be enamored with you.

**You tend to notice** the people, objects, activities, settings and experiences that evoke love, passion, and sensuality, particularly anything beautiful, romantic, aesthetic, or having an idealized quality. You may miss the importance of things that are merely functional, or things or people lacking in beauty, charm, or grace.

**You want to be seen as** attractive (physically and in every other way) and loveable. You do everything possible to look attractive and accessible to those you court and even to those whose attentions you may eventually need to spurn.

**Actions and qualities that you may find beneficial:**

- Clarifying values about sexual expression and friendship; maintaining good boundaries.

- Expressing sensuousness in all aspects of life, including everyday experiences such as the aroma of coffee or the songs of birds.

- Making a long-term commitment to care about others and their well–being even if the relationship, friendship, or project does not last.

- Cultivating a sense of identity and self-esteem that is independent of whether or not you love or are loved.

- Balancing the virtues of the Lover with those of the Seeker.

**If the Lover is one of your lowest scores,** you may do one or more of the following (check any that apply):

- ○ Find it difficult to be truly intimate with anyone or to commit to them.

- ○ Have an aversion to sexuality, nudity, or people with sexual orientations different from yours.

- ○ Not care much about beauty, sensuality, or having lovely experiences.

- ○ Laugh or smirk at the term "lover" if used to describe anyone you know.

- ○ You may not have yet had the deep experience of loving anyone or anything.

- ○ You have been taught that love makes you too vulnerable or that sexual love is demeaning, dirty, or dangerous.

# NOTES

**DESTROYER**

*Long ago, the god Hun Hunahpú (the Pre-Columbian Mayan god of maize) descended into the underworld realm of Zibalba, where he was defeated and killed by the twin lords of death. These lords then placed the head of the sacrificed god in the branches of a tree. The moment the head touched the tree, it instantly sprouted abundant foliage and enough fruit for all.*

*Later, a young maiden visited the tree, as she had heard how miraculous it was. As she reached for some fruit, Hunahpú spit in her hand, impregnating her and saying, "In my saliva and spittle I have given you my descendants. Go up, then, to the surface of the earth, that you may not die. Believe in my words that it will be so."*

*The maiden had twins who became great and joyous ballplayers, as their father had been before them. The lords of death challenged them to a contest. These playful Hero twins cheerfully survived all sorts of trials and even death (the House of Cold, the House of Jaguars, the House of Fire, the House of Knives). Eventually, they willingly jumped into a bonfire. After they were dead, their bones were ground up and thrown into a river. But they were miraculously resurrected. Realizing that they were immortal, they began to astound others by doing all sorts of tricks, including killing each other in assorted ways and coming right back to life. The lords of death become jealous of their fun and ability and begged to die too. The Hero twins killed them but did not allow their resurrection. The Hero twins then found their father and restored him to life. It is the resurrected Hun Hunahpú who created the World Tree that links heaven and earth and is the axis of creation, making our world possible.*

From: *Popol Vuh: The Book of the People* by Delia Goetz and Sylvanus Griswold Morley, translated by Adrian Recino.

Although most modern cultures fear the actions of the Destroyer, this story is one of many myths and folk tales that show us that new life can be achieved through death and loss. It shows that death is not only unavoidable, but also necessary to life and creativity. In this story, the god could not have created the World Tree, and with it the world itself, without having suffered and died first.

**The archetypal character:** The Destroyer character can be seen as a victim (who experiences tragedy or loss and then has to rebuild his or her life), as an initiate (who willingly accepts an experience of metamorphosis), as an outlaw (who breaks unjust rules like Zorro or Robin Hood), or as a revolutionary (who actively undermines the order to make way for something better).

**The archetypal plot:** Destroyer stories are often about unforeseen disruption or destruction (external). They can also depict the process of learning to let go of possessions, situations, relationships, and habits. Generally, there is no assumption that someone should be saving you from these problems, unless the story also has Orphan elements. The Destroyer offers the opportunity to trust the process of letting go, whether chosen or not, as part of a process of metamorphosis. In the story's positive form, metamorphosis leads to something much better. In ironic or tragic form, metamorphosis fails to happen.

**Other stories that primarily concern the Destroyer:**

- The whole genre of horror stories, those about monsters, deranged or villainous people who do unspeakable things to others (*Alien* or *The Ring*).

- Stories of natural or manmade disasters where people are killed, wounded, or maimed (*The Perfect Storm* or *The Constant Gardener*), or stories in which faith is lost (Stephen Crane's *The Open Boat and Other Stories*).

- Cautionary tales (*The Rime of the Ancient Mariner*) where someone lives to tell the tale so as to warn others about how to avoid such destruction.

- Narratives of letting go, in which someone abandons (or renounces) or even destroys aspects of his or her life that were once important (*Drinking: A Love Story*).

- Tales using the Phoenix concept that involve people rebuilding their lives or their faith after tragedies (*The Shipping News, The Horse Whisperer, The Divine Secrets of the Ya Ya Sisterhood*, or Hemingway's tale of *The Old Man and the Sea*.) The Phoenix is a beautiful bird of Egyptian mythology who, when it feels death approach, builds a nest of aromatic cinnamon branches and sets it on fire. After being consumed by the fire, a new Phoenix rises from the ashes.

- Outlaw stories, where an individual or a group breaks unjust laws (or thrives outside the law); tales about people who risk or give their lives to create a better order; or whistle-blowers who risk their jobs to stop unethical practices (*Erin Brockovich, The Insider*).

- Inspiring stories about people such as Thoreau on Walden Pond, who simplify their lives and discover that eliminating activities and possessions often brings greater richness of life. This destruction can be either figurative or literal.

**Imagery:** Destroyer imagery is symbolized by the dark of night, black holes, Halloween, monsters, the Grim Reaper, hooded and threatening figures—all reflecting a cultural fear of this archetype. Other, less frightening images include fall leaves, objects dropped into bodies of water, a wave of goodbye, weeding the garden, pruning a tree, or cleaning out a closet.

**Gifts:** The wisdom fostered by the Destroyer experience includes discernment about when to hold on and when to let go and about how to manage the terror of going into the unknown. When people move beyond the fear of death, loss, or change, they gain an incredible kind of freedom that can take the form of the ability to live fully in the moment, the capacity to take risks without undue stress, the willingness to risk failure in order to create deeper knowledge, and the wisdom to flow with life's changes (such as growing older). When we make friends with the Destroyer, we no longer need to shrink in fear, holding on to what we have (no matter how negative). We begin to see that it is possible to trust the unknown.

**Social support:** People need places to fall apart and come back together, places that are not so much about fixing problems as about providing rituals for acceptance, letting go, and then making new choices. People also need assistance to take inventory of what in their life is "dead" and what needs to be revived or sacrificed so that vitality and zest for life can re-emerge. In order to honor legacies and keep others alive through memories, people need times and places to share stories of those who are no longer with us, whether living far away or through death.

**In nature:** The jack pine prefers sunlight, and its humpbacked cones open only after being heated to a couple of hundred degrees. Thus it thrives only after the forest is devastated by fire; and its shade and soft, easily decayed wood provide the conditions for new woodland. Nature reflects a continuous cycle of birth, life, and death—as a simple walk in the woods illustrates: sprouting plants and decomposing leaves, birds eating insects, mushrooms living off decaying logs. Stars and even whole galaxies are created and then eventually die. Destruction is inherent in the food chain as every living organism has a natural predator.

**In spirituality:** Although the details differ, virtually every religion has ways to help people overcome the fear of death and loss and to find ways to trust life. Many religions also talk about "dying" to an old way of being (in Christianity it is a sinful way of being; in Buddhism, an ego-oriented, desire-based consciousness) and moving into a new way of being that is more moral and fulfilling. In this way, lesser modes of being are sacrificed to the attainment of higher ways of being. Many religions, moreover, teach that even physical death is not the end, but can be followed by resurrection or reincarnation.

**As leaders:** People with good access to the Destroyer archetype tend to be good at re-engineering or redesigning organizations, ending unproductive programs, and firing unproductive workers. Ideally, they demonstrate powers of discernment to keep them from metaphorically cutting down the trees in winter (because they cannot distinguish between temporary and permanent unproductiveness). These types of leaders also do their best to minimize the hurt, anxiety, and fear that accompanies the change process in organizations.

...................................................................

If the Destroyer is active in your life,
you may want to let go or to cut your losses.

...................................................................

**At your best** (now or when you fulfill your potential), you know how to deal with loss gracefully, letting go and moving on. You are also able to weed out old habits, possessions, and relationships and phase out projects and activities that are no longer productive or fulfilling. Over time, you may have come to acknowledge the complex interrelationship between experiencing destruction you do not choose, and deciding to end something. For example, after tragedy or misfortune strikes, you may have to let go of both possessions and lifestyle in order to re-create your life. (Consider the difficult choices faced by the victims of hurricane Katrina or the tsunami that devastated parts of Sumatra.) Even ending a self-destructive habit requires change in order for a person to overcome it. And, if you take strong action to end a marriage, blow the whistle on injustice, or end an unproductive endeavor, you may have to sacrifice a great deal in the process.

**You may want to guard against** lashing out or harming others. You may rationalize breaking ethical or legal rules because "the end justifies the means." You may need to guard against behaviors that are emotionally or physically violent or that break the law or harm yourself or another.

**When problems emerge,** especially when destruction threatens what you hold most dear, you may feel confused and afraid, triggering some deep and complicated questions. However, as you grapple with these questions, you gain the wisdom to change what you can and accept what cannot be changed, opening yourself to being transformed in the experience. When you identify things that are wrong in the world, you may take on the role of the outlaw or the revolutionary, breaking the rules or even the law, if necessary, to put an end to injustice or harmful practices.

**Others may appreciate** and even be fascinated by the way your suffering or your outlaw/revolutionary activities place you a bit outside the regular world. They may, however, avoid being with you out of a superstitious belief that misfortune is contagious or out of fear of sharing the consequences of outlaw or revolutionary behaviors.

**You tend to notice** and focus on the pending crisis or destructive force, on strategies for maintaining equilibrium and just getting through the situation, and on the means to bring the problem to an end. You may also notice the injustice of the situation and try to figure out ways to remedy this unfairness, either through compensation ("Living well is the best revenge," or "I'll get what is coming to me") or revolution ("I'll change the world").

**You want to be seen as** whole, even when you are going through difficult times, so you may hesitate to share the immensity of what you are going through. You may also want others to understand that you do not mean to be ruthless or unkind just because you need to cut things out of your life that no longer work for you.

**Actions or qualities that you may find beneficial:**

- Having a metaphysical view that accounts for life's injustices.

- A clear sense of personal ethics ("if you are going to live outside the law, you have to be honest").

- A study of the natural processes of birth, maturation, and death; an attention to the consequences of your actions for yourself and others; and a commitment to minimizing the pain involved in change.

- Balancing the virtues of the Destroyer with that of the Creator.

**READ ME!**

Note that the items on the PMAI® assessment focus on those aspects of the Destroyer that are the result of unwanted change rather than the aspects of the Destroyer that measure change made by active choice.

○ ○ ○

**If the Destroyer is one of your lowest scores**, you may do one or more of the following (check any that apply):

○ Feel unprepared to deal with death or loss.

○ Hold on to things and people long after they have lost meaning or value for you.

○ See yourself as essentially unchanging (that's just who I am).

○ Never have experienced any significant unwanted change.

○ Have been taught that you should always be able to keep your life under control.

## CREATOR

*In the beginning, Llmater, a maiden and daughter of the ether, lived alone in the great expanse of heaven. Llmater was sad for she was lonely. So she decided to descend to the firmament, landing on the ocean, where she was tossed to and fro by powerful waves which impregnated her with the union of power and beauty. As she became large with child, she could not even rise above the surface of the water, and she labored there for seven hundred years until finally she began weeping at her fate, praying that she would be delivered of this child.*

*Just at this time a duck appeared looking for a place to nest. The compassionate maiden, and now a water-mother, lifted her knees just enough out of the water to provide the duck a place to lay her eggs in safety. As the duck warmed her seven eggs, the water beneath her became hot, until it started to burn the maiden, who threw off the eggs. The eggs shattered and then reconfigured on the ocean floor in great beauty to form the lower vault of earth and the upper vault of heaven. The white of the eggs became the moon and the yolk the sun. Then swimming about, the water-mother created all the rest of the earth, but still she remained undelivered.*

*Within her Wainamoinen, the first man—a hero and singer—remained trapped, increasingly impatient to be born. He was a full adult and yearned to walk on the dry land which his mother had created and to enjoy the sunshine and moonlight. He began to pray for his deliverance out of the womb, which he came to see as a dark prison, but no one helped. Finally, he took things into his own hands, making his way through the birth canal and out into the water. In the water, he rested for seven years until he finally stepped onto the dry land and walked in the crisp air, singing under the moon and the constellation of the Great Bear.*

From the Finnish creation myth, *The Kalevala* by Elias Lönnrot, translated by John Martin Crawford (1888).

Implicit in this story is the tension between the more "heroic" creative urge of Wainamoinen and Llmater's more organic process of birthing. Although once Llmater is heated by the fire, she also creates in a more intentional and dynamic way. In this myth, we see a process involving five elements (ether, water, fire/heat, earth, and air) which contrasts the urgency of the desire to birth (and be birthed) against the reality that the creation of anything truly magnificent takes time.

**The archetypal character:** The Creator character can be an artist whose work is to create literature, art, music, or some other artistic form; an entrepreneur, inventor, or innovator; or anyone who uses imagination and creativity in work or daily life.

**The archetypal plot:** The Creator story line typically includes a foil for the Creator—one or more people who have little regard for the creative process. They may counsel or even pressure the Creator to live a more ordinary, conformist life and to attempt to succeed in more traditional ways. The Creator thus needs to find a way to express his or her own creative vision in ways that others appreciate and value. Other stories that primarily concern the Creator:

- Stories of struggling artists who (while staying true to their art) grapple with poverty, not being appreciated, or even became addicted to drugs or alcohol (the movie *Ray* about Ray Charles, or *Walk the Line* about Johnny Cash). In the positive form, Creator archetypes eventually triumph and gain success. In the tragic form, they exploit or even give up their art. Sometimes they suffer in poverty because they will not compromise their standards or allow their creativity to be co-opted by others (*Amadeus*, about the life of Mozart).

- Narratives about ordinary people who change their lives by reflecting on them. (Abilene and the other woman in the book *The Help*, who raised white children in the racially conflicted South.) These women changed their lives by telling the collective story of their lives.

- Narratives, such as *Fried Green Tomatoes* or *Big Fish*, where the creative act of telling a story becomes a life-changing force in the life of another character.

- Tales of artists, inventors, entrepreneurs, and other creative people who have the imagination to envision something admirable and have, or develop, the skill to make that vision a reality.

**Imagery:** Birth, the sun rising or any other image of beginnings, the picture on the ceiling of the Sistine Chapel of Adam's hand rising to touch God's, God as Creator, flowers opening, the beginning of spring, all forms of art.

**Gifts:** The Creator fuels innovation, artistry, creativity, imagination, and anything new that emerges in the world.

**Social support:** This archetype is encouraged when the arts are supported and when ordinary people have access to experiencing and understanding the arts. It is also supported when craft is a natural part of life and is acknowledged as an important aspect of human development. Most importantly, creativity flourishes when we move beyond the dualistic idea of the great artist or innovator as separate from everyone else to a mind-set of helping everyone find his or her own way of being creative. Society evolves when each person lives his or her life in a way that reflects personal uniqueness.

**In nature:** Whether we look to the sky or on the earth, we see incredible variety. Nature is creative and prolific, providing all sorts of species that continue to evolve and change. The gestation period involved in any birthing–whether of a seed germinating, a bird in the egg, or a fetus in the womb–seems relatively invisible until the dramatic moment when the plant sprouts through the earth, the egg cracks open, or the baby is born. Creation is all around us in nature.

**In spirituality:** In most spiritual traditions, God (or a collection of gods or a universal force of some kind) is honored as the Creator of all life and is also seen as present in all people, who can create their own lives (and artistry) out of their connection with spirit, or with the common good. Conversely, people can also make mischief by creating out of their own egocentric willfulness (present in cautionary tales about those granted three wishes who lack the wisdom to wish intelligently).

**As leaders:** The Creator is entrepreneurial, innovative, and unorthodox and can create new or innovative products, business, organizational ways of operating, or new frontiers of knowledge. The Creator leader may craft an organization like an artist crafts a painting, story, or song. They move from inspiration to structures that can hold and reflect that inspiration. Or the leader may initiate even more organic change, birthing new potentials within the organization that are just waiting to be delivered.

> If the Creator is active in your life, you
> assume what can be imagined can be created.

**At your best** (now or when you fulfill your potential), you are highly imaginative and even inspired, and your skill level allows you to create with ease. You have moments when the ideas just flow and creativity seems effortless. You have a wonderfully developed aesthetic sense and surround yourself with things that reflect your taste. You have the potential to create your own life as a work of art so that you avoid the ordinary, the shallow, and the mundane, opting for more satisfying ways of life–even if this means that others do not always understand why you live the way you do.

**You may want to guard against** the Creator's tendency to reduce life to raw material for art (as in a cartoon depicting a writer who keeps one hand on the keyboard as he is making love), robbing life of the joy of felt experience. The Creator also may become overwhelmed as a result of taking on too many projects. Like weeds that kill a garden, too many projects can sap the joy out of an otherwise great life. When the inner critic gets out of control, Creators may undermine their own confidence and that of others.

**When problems emerge,** you seek inspiration to develop a clear vision of how you want to remedy them, to decide what you want to create to put in their place, or to choose what other innovative steps you might take. You may divert yourself by undertaking some satisfying creative project, believing, often correctly, that the answer to how to handle the problem will come to you in the process.

**Others may appreciate** and even envy your imagination and taste. However, they may have no idea how much dedication and hard work is involved in creating anything of real worth, minimizing what the outcome costs you. They may even see you as elitist or eccentric, perhaps even immoral (you know those artists!) and someone not to be trusted.

**You tend to notice** the need for new inventions or interpretations. You also focus on the resources that help you innovate and on ways to enhance your skills. You know that if you open your eyes wide enough, you will find what you need to be successful. You also have a highly developed critical sense and generally notice every flaw in what you and others do, which could lead you to feel inadequate to the task and dissatisfied with life.

**You want to be seen as** grounded, practical, and having the ability to create something the world needs, so you may avoid doing things that make you seem like a stereotypically wild-eyed, crazy artist.

### Actions or qualities that you may find beneficial:

- Taming your inner critic so that you become more appropriately critical of others and yourself.

- Remembering that anything worth doing takes time to complete.

- Moving from an ego-oriented focus on whether what you do is good enough to an attitude of service, being a channel for the muse or the vision to be expressed.

    ○ Balancing artistry with being a responsible, thoughtful person (avoiding the trap of excusing self-indulgence).

    ○ Balancing the virtues of the Creator with those of the Destroyer.

**If the Creator is one of your lowest scores,** you may do one or more of the following (check any that apply):

    ○ Get stuck in a rut.

    ○ Feel frustrated that your creative self cannot be expressed.

    ○ Lack the ability to imagine ways to do things other than what you have already seen and experienced.

    ○ Daydream, but never act on those daydreams, even though you would like to.

    ○ Have never yet had any reason to want to create anything new.

    ○ Have been taught that creative people are flighty, poor, unsuccessful, untrustworthy, or immoral.

# NOTES

**RULER**

*Long ago and far away a kingdom had become a wasteland, experiencing not only famine but a sense of malaise that dispirited everyone in it. As in many times and places in the world, the people of this country believed that the health of the kingdom was dependent upon the health of the monarch. They understood that things were not working in their land because the king was both physically and mentally wounded. However, a legend predicted this dreary time: the ailing king, and a visiting knight who, without knowing the legend, would ask two magical questions which would heal the king and restore the prosperity of the country.*

*Meanwhile, in King Arthur's castle a young knight named Parsifal was being trained for knighthood. He was a rather naive fellow, brought up in the provinces. He had so many questions (just as children do today) that he was told never again to ask any unnecessary questions. Over time he became a great and accomplished knight and soon found himself traveling to the ailing king's land. He was invited to dine with the king and was terribly curious about the nature of the king's suffering and of what appeared to be a magical grail that provided everyone at the table the food and drink they most loved. However, Parsifal did not ask any questions because he had been warned not to, and he was trying to be a good knight. Everyone was incredibly let down, and they saddled his horse and sent him on his way. Years later he learned what he had failed to do. And even though he thought it was unlikely that he could successfully heal the king, he went back and asked the two questions that originally burned in his heart. With genuine feeling and sympathy, he asked: "What ails you, Uncle?" and "Who serves the grail?" Ultimately, the king was healed and the kingdom restored to prosperity.*

Adapted from *Myths to Live By* and *Transformation of Myth through Time* by Joseph Campbell and *The Complete Romances of Chrétien de Troyes* by David Staines.

According to Joseph Campbell, Parsifal's two questions can restore the king (and Parsifal) to health. The first question opens the heart and acknowledges genuine sympathy and relationship. As the grail is sent from God, the second question reminds the king that his suffering comes from being disconnected from his soul. When he is reconnected to that deeper self, he comes back into health and power. Implicit in this story, and in the archetype of the Ruler, is an understanding of the interconnectedness of the inner and outer worlds. When things are right inside us, it is easier to right the world outside ourselves.

**The archetypal character:** The Ruler archetype can be seen in anyone with authority and in individuals or groups that shoulder responsibilities in families or organizations. Those who take such responsibilities seriously and learn to perform them well typically gain power, authority, and both privilege and temptations. The Ruler is faced with the decision to take advantage of this power for personal gain or to use it wisely for the common good. The Ruler archetype offers the potential to claim authority and order life in ways that reflect personal values.

**The archetypal plot:** Accepting stewardship for a family, a group, an organization, or a nation is a big responsibility, and there is a whole genre of biographies, historic events, movies, and books that offer examples of this archetype in action. The initial situation generally includes a "kingdom" in jeopardy (chaos, misrule, and/or a scarcity of resources and talent) and then shows how the leader succeeds (or tragically fails) to turn around the situation. If successful, he or she fosters order, harmony, and shared prosperity. (King Arthur is the perennial mythic example of the Ruler archetype.)

Other stories that primarily concern the Ruler:

- Stories in which someone accepts or denies responsibility for a kingdom (*Elizabeth*, *The Lion King*, or *Prince Hal* in Shakespeare's *Henry IV*). Stories about ordinary people willing to limit their freedoms in order to take on responsibilities as parents, citizens, neighbors, workers, and leaders.

- Tragic Ruler stories show how the arrogance (hubris), corruption and/or despotism of the leader threatens or destroys the family, group, company, or state (most Greek tragedies). Other examples of the tragic Ruler include stories of gossip and rumor about the behavior of celebrities (as featured in *People Magazine* and British tabloids). Ruler stories can also show redemption (Martha Stewart's post prison efforts to rebuild her business).

- Ruler-in-exile stories (*Robin Hood*) or stories about revolutionary leaders restoring a rightful leader or way of life (*The Constant Gardener*).

- Stories that show a flawed leader renouncing power are deeply mythic and demonstrate the ancient belief that in a symbiotic relationship between the Ruler and the kingdom, the kingdom cannot thrive with a Ruler who has lost his or her vitality. Thus, infirm or impotent Rulers must be sacrificed when they lose their power (James George Frazer's *The Golden Bough* or Saul Bellow's *Henderson the Rain King*). The promise and hope is that a new just and able leader (or leadership team) will restore peace, justice, effectiveness, and prosperity for all.

- Exemplary Ruler plotlines show how great leaders can move people to do their best with ripple effects that ennoble the rest of the community, or even the world. Consider, for example, Nelson Mandela's ability to forgive and work with the same people who sent him to prison for twenty-seven years. His just and benevolent behavior as a leader facilitated a more peaceful end to apartheid in South Africa.

**Imagery:** The grandeur associated with royalty, expensive clothing, ornate rooms, imposing buildings (which may have columns and other grand touches), square and rectangular forms, deep purple and other beautiful rich colors, people moving in slow, stately ways.

**Gifts:** Gifts of the Ruler include claiming one's own power and authority, living by strong personal values, taking on responsibilities, being aware of how one is seen, dealing with the politics and leadership that are a part of most endeavors.

**Social supports:** A society needs ordinary people as well as politicians and corporate leaders to organize and rule as good citizens. From school-age on, people need to assume responsibilities and understand the value of leadership for their own development and for that of society. People need to understand the interaction between what they think and do and what consequences such actions have on others in a society or organization.

**In nature:** Ruler energy in nature is reflected in natural laws that when ignored may produce dire results. Think of people who build homes in natural environments that are known for floods, mudslides, or fires, and the personal disasters that can result from such decisions. The success of Rulers can depend on making good decisions, putting the right policies or systems in place that reflect the principles behind the laws of nature.

**In spirituality:** The Ruler finds spiritual meaning in taking responsibility for the good of the whole. In ancient times, the doctrine of the divine right of kings meant that the monarch spoke for God. In modern life, the authority of the Ruler archetype is about an ability to stay connected with both the divine within and with the people affected by one's decisions and actions. The good Ruler can be seen as trying to reflect heaven on earth, fostering attitudes and systems that reflect the highest and best potential within any situation.

**As leaders:** Rulers are good at putting structures, policies, and procedures in place that make life easier and more efficient. They also excel at networking and at moving along business and political processes. Rulers attend well to ceremonial events and act responsibly under unpleasant circumstances. In addition, they are responsible even for problems they did not create.

If the Ruler is active in your life, you
assume that you should exercise control.

**At your best** (now or when you fulfill your potential), you step up to the plate to take control when things are in disarray. Like the good king, queen, president, boss, or parent, you reign for the good of those who follow you, so that your highly developed sense of responsibility and order benefits everyone. You know that healthy social systems do not just happen. Someone needs to shoulder the responsibility to create them. You are not only willing to be that person, you also recruit others and groom or coach them, knowing that the more you are willing to claim your own power, the better you are at empowering others.

**You may want to guard against** the Ruler's tendency to be dictatorial or to use the Ruler's position to enhance status, prestige, or financial means at the expense of responsibilities. Rulers also may misinterpret differences of opinion as threats to power and/or put too many rules in place, thus creating "catch-22" situations where nothing gets accomplished.

**When problems emerge,** your natural response is to put in place policies, procedures, and systems, not only to solve this problem and all similar ones, but also to avoid such difficulties in the future. You also monitor these systems and resist those "loose cannons" that get carried away by wild ideas that might throw a monkey wrench in your well-oiled machine.

**Others may appreciate** how you take charge and get things done. They also may envy and undermine your authority and, in response to it, become passive aggressive, overtly oppositional, or competitive, or flatter you to get in your good graces.

**You tend to notice** the tools and trappings of power and where the source of authority lies. You also know how to use status, image, and prestige to intensify your power, and hence you are attentive to how you appear to others and to context appropriateness (for example, not overdressing while visiting a poverty program). You may fail to notice the important input of people who have little or no status.

**You want to be seen as** so thoroughly in charge that others naturally follow you, but you avoid doing anything too harsh so as not to seem cruel and unfeeling.

### Actions or qualities that you may find beneficial:

- Having a commitment to governing for the good of all.

- Sharing power and encouraging as much self-determinism as possible in others.

- Remembering that you cannot make people do anything, but you can inspire them by sharing a worthy vision of outcomes that take their interests into account.

- Modeling the behaviors you wish others to exhibit.

- Balancing the virtues of the Ruler with those of the Magician.

**If Ruler is one of your lowest scores,** you may do one or more of the following (check any that apply):

- ○ Have trouble being responsible or doing your duty.

- ○ Have difficulty putting systems and orderly habits in place.

- ○ Live by others' rules and values rather than your own.

- ○ Feel irritated at people who are bossy, take charge, or order you or others around.

- ○ Have had little or no chance to be responsible for yourself or others, or to take charge.

- ○ Have been taught to think (or you decided based on an experience with a despot) that people who act like Rulers are bad.

# NOTES

## MAGICIAN

*For most of the 400 years that the Outer Banks of North Carolina has been occupied by European settlers, it has been a remote and desolate outcropping. By the early 1900s, following the publicity of the Wright brothers' famous flights, summer tourists began arriving by boat from Norfolk and Elizabeth City. Despite the construction of a few grand old hotels and cottages on the sounds, many "bankers" (descendants of those early settlers) continued to eke a living from the sea, living in isolated communities or in remote huts in the gnarled woods. In one cedar-sided cabin lived an old woman and her black cats. She went by the name of Miss Mabe, and it was said that she "had the sight." Children would search for coins beneath the piers and plank walkways, then, unbeknownst to their parents, and make their way to Miss Mabe's cottage. For a coin of any denomination, she would tell them their future. She always foretold pleasant things for the children—candy, fishing trips—and, surprisingly, many of the events foretold came to pass. A rickety pier snaked its way from Miss Mabe's house into the sound. There she would sit and gaze over the water. It was the custom of returning fishermen to throw several fish from the day's catch onto her dock; and Miss Mabe would call out a blessing for the man and his boat. But occasionally, a returning fisherman would be preoccupied and neglect to share his catch. Within twelve hours the wind would shift. A gale would blow out of the northeast, and the boats could not go out. The fishermen would send a delegation to apologize and implore Miss Mabe to change the wind. Miss Mabe never promised to change the wind back, and she would accept no payment from the delegation. She would tell them she was just a poor widow woman, but she would see what could be done. Invariably the wind would shift back, bringing with it an even greater bounty of fish.*

Story excerpted and retold from "The Witch of Nag's Head Woods" in *Legends of the Outer Banks and Tar Heel Tidewater* by C. H. Whedbee.

This story raises important questions about magical figures: to what degree are they doing magic versus to what degree do people ascribe magic to them based on a belief that they are controlling events? Like the Ruler, their power comes from the synchronistic relationship between their inner state of consciousness and outer reality. The story of the rainmaker is helpful here. A rainmaker would be called to a village during a drought. He would enter into a home, meditate, and get his consciousness aligned with the place. Then the rain would fall. The magician seemingly conjures the miraculous through a deeper understanding of how much of our world is determined by our perception. By altering his own and others' perceptions, the Magician alters the known world.

**The archetypal character:** The characters from stories and myth that come to mind as examples of the Magician are Merlin from Arthurian legends, Yoda in *Star Wars*, Mary Poppins, the witches and the wizard in *The Wizard of Oz*, Harry Potter, or any indigenous shaman or medicine woman. Typically, these characters are not at the center of power. Rather, they are on the sidelines, or they help leaders succeed by providing vision. They bring out the potential in others and expose people to empowering esoteric secrets about how the world really works. Sometimes, as in Prospero, a character in Shakespeare's *Tempest*, the Magician and the Ruler exist in one person who uses magical wisdom to right the kingdom. The Magician within offers the opportunity to change your outer life to realize your hopes and dreams by first changing inner thoughts and attitudes.

**The archetypal plot:** Something is wrong. A person is ill and needs to be healed. Things have broken down, and need to be set right. The Magician intercedes to heal or to transform the situation, but does not generally aspire to positions of overt power and authority. Rather, the Magician archetype prefers to be on the sidelines, retaining freedom and time for the inner work that gives him or her power. However, when Ruler energy is also present or when circumstances demand it, the Magician may take on the mantel of direct power in the world.

### Other stories that primarily concern the Magician:

- Stories such as the Harry Potter series, that focus on the growth and development of the Magician, who typically comes from difficult circumstances, having experienced significant wounding (for Harry the loss of his parents and the scar on his forehead inflicted by the dreaded Voldemort). Their power to help others comes from having first healed themselves (Ursula LeGu in *Earthsea Trilogy* or Black Elk in *Black Elk Speaks*).

- Visionary stories, such as the ones about Merlin, the wizard in the Arthurian legends, who shows others how to develop a sense of what might be accomplished and how to implement that vision. Sometimes, as with the heroine of the movie *Chocolat*, they heal the community and move from the sidelines to a more prominent role.

- Cautionary tales about Magicians who abuse their power, going over to the dark side, such as Voldemort in the *Harry Potter* series or Darth Vader in the *Star Wars* series.

- Spiritual narratives about the miraculous abilities of saints and mystics from a variety of spiritual traditions. These characters connect directly with their divine nature and are able to heal the sick, solve seemingly insurmountable problems, preside over rituals to restore harmony and love, or connect people with God or their own divine natures.

- Salvation narratives whereby a person accepts grace through divine intervention, resulting in a miraculous change in life, or where a change in consciousness, generally assisted by spiritual help, allows someone to escape the laws of fate, which might require them to suffer the consequences of sinful or ill-advised behaviors.

**Imagery:** As a master of the laws of nature, the Magician archetype is often evoked by images from nature–not so much your everyday meadow, but craggy peaks, expanse of oceans, or the night sky. Images of power are often common, such as lightning or a comet, as are views of the world that are usually out of our reach because they are too small (microscopic life) or too big or far away (other galaxies). Figures of Magicians are rarely "dressed for success." Think of the simple attire worn by Jesus or Gandhi or the flowing robes of mythic Magicians in stories such as *The Lord of the Rings* or the *Harry Potter* series.

**Gifts:** The Magician serves as a catalyst who has real power to shape and influence events, not through positional power, but through charisma, influence, and the triumph of character over circumstances. Often the Magician understands natural laws that others do not, and so appears to have supernatural powers.

**Social support:** Magicians often live on the edges of society, as most contemporary societies focus only on the surface of things, and Magicians seek to understand forces in depth. The Berlin Wall coming down, apartheid ending in South Africa, and individuals forgiving those who have harmed them are examples of the Magician at work in social situations. The success of the Harry Potter series shows us that children are hungry for magic, and although often less ready to admit it, so are adults. The Magician archetype, however, is unlikely to emerge in a positive form in a society unless there is sustained education about inner life as well as implications (and integration) of the old and new sciences for understanding existence and purpose.

**In nature:** The magic of birth, the big bang, the mysterious appearance of solar systems or the evolution of human beings are examples of the Magician archetype in nature. Think of the magic of subatomic particles—quarks, neutrinos, and other invisible phenomena—that are so difficult to understand. Think of the experience of transforming an old idea into a new experience.

**In spirituality:** Magicians are willing and able to make (or allow) miracles to occur, but they see them as coming through them from a divine source. Opening to allow miracles is thus a spiritual practice. When things go wrong in their outer world, Magicians know to go inward to pray or meditate to right their inner world; knowing that when they become different, they will act differently, and events will then shift—not just causally, but synchronistically in a way that cannot be completely explained.

**As leaders:** Magical leaders are visionaries who energize others by inspiring them to be true to their deeper values and to work together to make a wonderfully transformative dream come true (Martin Luther King, Jr.). Magical leaders are good at fostering flexible structures and attitudes of personal responsibility and responsiveness in everyone. They create synergistic partnerships and networks whose whole is greater than the sum of their parts. They excel at leading whole movements. They tend not to micromanage, but to first get alignment on a vision and then allow people to have freedom to make local decisions about how that vision might be realized.

> If the Magician is active in your life,
> you assume that perception defines reality.

**At your best** (now or when you fulfill your potential), you are a charismatic, transformative, and healing presence who knows how to unite people behind a common vision and make that vision a reality. You understand that the structures of consciousness govern what happens in life, and you are highly self-aware. You may use prayer, meditation, psychotherapy, or other methods to be certain that you are mentally clear and living in a way that is in keeping with your purpose. Most of all, you believe that seemingly miraculous events can happen if human beings just get smart enough to understand more about how the science of nature, the mind, and the spirit work together.

**You may want to guard against** the Magician's tendency to get hooked by gurus who promise easy magical solutions, or you may fall prey to the temptation to set yourself up as a guru. The Magician can use charisma to manipulate others and overwhelm them with extremely high expectations. The Magician may also underestimate what it takes to consistently pull rabbits out of hats.

**When problems emerge,** you respond first by changing your own attitudes, expanding your perspectives, and adjusting your behavior to create ripple effects that may shift the whole system. You also work to reframe the situation in ways that help you or others see solutions that otherwise might be overlooked. You trust that when your intent is clear and pure, things will work out.

**Others may appreciate** your charisma and vision; they also may dismiss you as a flake or fear that you will set yourself up as a guru, actually or metaphorically wearing white robes.

**You tend to notice** serendipity, synchronicity (meaningful coincidences), the interrelationship of events and seemingly disparate parts of a system, the ripple effects that emerge from seemingly small changes (The Butterfly Effect), and the ways in which attitudes affect outcomes. You are also keenly interested in how things work from a metaphysical or spiritual, as well as scientific perspective. Yet sometimes you may miss the obvious and seem lacking in common sense.

**You like to be seen as** a visionary but also as mysterious and even a little removed and unnerving. While this makes for some loneliness, it also contributes to your power. You may prefer a role on the sidelines, as an internal or external consultant, for example, rather than as the chief executive officer of an organization.

### Actions or qualities that you may find beneficial:

- Taking a scientific approach to understanding how the world works, studying natural processes and tracking what actually works, not just what sounds good.

- Doing inner work that fosters awareness of psychological forces, heals wounds from one's early life, and keeps you self-aware and aligned with your sense of life purpose.

- Being aware of how other people think and act, without needing to change them.

- Staying grounded through routine work, being in nature, and experiencing the joys of sensuality.

○ Balancing the virtues of the Magician with those of the Ruler.

**If the Magician is one of your lowest scores,** you may do one or more of the following (check any that apply):

○ Find it difficult to develop a vision of the future or to use charisma to galvanize collective efforts.

○ Think that everything that is not explained by reason or by linear causality is nonsense.

○ Have disdain for people who believe in miracles or that seek out esoteric knowledge about how the world and people work.

○ Not have been in any situation where noticing synchronicity (or meaningful coincidences between what is happening in the inner and outer worlds) would be helpful to you.

○ Have been taught not to believe in magic, miracles, or anyone claiming to do anything outside the bounds of what is commonly understood (you may have even been taught that such people are be evil, deluded, or con artists).

**SAGE**

*Once a poor distraught Jewish man sought an audience with the rabbi. "Holy Rabbi, my life is terrible. I cannot manage another day!"*

*"What seems to be the problem?" inquired the rabbi.*

*"I am poor, and I live in a one room hut with my wife, my six children, and my in-laws. There is no room, and we quarrel."*

*The rabbi pondered for a moment, then asked "have you any animals?"*

*"Yes," answered the man, "a goat, some chickens, and a cow."*

*"Then take the animals into your house, and God will help you."*

*The man did as he was told, but returned a few days later. "Holy Rabbi, things are awful. I did as you told me, and now the chickens are squawking and fouling the table, and there is not even room to sleep."*

*"Then remove the chickens," advised the rabbi.*

*The man did as he was told, but returned again. "Holy Rabbi, you have made my life unbearable. The goat eats our clothes and breaks everything."*

*The rabbi was thoughtful. "You must remove the goat," he advised.*

*The man returned yet again. "Holy Rabbi, the cow is always in our way, and she defecates on the floor. We work so hard to clean behind her we barely have time to speak to one another."*

*"You are right," admitted the rabbi. "Take out the cow."*

*A few days later the man returned. "Holy Rabbi, I want to thank you. The house is so clean and quiet, and we all get along so well. I feel blessed."*

"It Could Always Be Worse," a Jewish folktale retold from Jane Yolen in *Favorite Folktales from Around the World.*

While archetypes like the Lover and the Magician help us realize our desires, the Sage helps us let go of what we think we want in order to accept reality as it is. Indeed, as one Sage put it: "Don't fight reality. It always wins." This story illustrates the inherent tension within the Sage archetype between the desire to understand reality as it is and the knowledge that we see reality through our own lens, and therefore our sense of reality is relative to our experience.

**The archetypal character:** The Sage may be a scholar, a spiritual teacher, or just someone (often older) who has learned from experience what to expect and what not to expect from life or from any situation. The motivation of the Sage is to find truth, or at least to move closer to satisfying his or her curiosity and inquiring mind. The Sage within offers the potential for wisdom and for the freedom that comes from learning the truth about what is real.

**The archetypal plot:** The genre of the Sage archetype is the mystery story. It begins with a fact or event that is curious and unexplained: a murder, an unexplained result in a lab, the discovery of ancient documents. Then the Sage archetype, represented as the scholar, sleuth, or wisdom figure undertakes a process for uncovering the truth. The consciousness of the Sage is reflected in academic writings, mystery stories, biographies, or histories that are tales of discoveries (Sherlock Holmes mysteries or Umberto Eco's *The Name of the Rose*).

### Other stories that primarily concern the Sage:

- Narratives that show someone learning to think, reflect, or figure things out. In adolescence, the Sage may be seen by other children as a geek, until adulthood when intellect results in great achievement.

- Stories about teachers and their impact on the young for good or ill (*The Prime of Miss Jean Brodie, Mona Lisa's Smile,* or *Mr. Holland's Opus*). These narratives also include wise oracles or guides who teach others how to succeed in their quests. In fairy tales, the Sage is represented by the wise old man or woman who provides advice and possibly a talisman.

- Detective stories about how an investigator, a scholar, or anyone else figures out what others have missed (the Miss Marple mysteries, *The Da Vinci Code*).

- Wisdom stories that show a person triumphing over their own thoughts (as in *A Beautiful Mind,* where John Nash overcomes mental illness by learning to know what thoughts he can trust and which he cannot). This type of Sage narrative is also exemplified by the Buddha and his understanding of the importance of moving past desire and even past thoughts to connect directly with a higher wisdom beyond the mind.

**Imagery:** Sage images include libraries, books, archives, spectacles, absent-minded professors, laboratories, and the workings of technology. When the Sage is crossed with the Magician, a crystal ball or other device used by oracles is a prominent image.

**Gifts:** The gifts of the Sage include intelligence, curiosity, an open mind, knowing where to find information, critical thinking, and the capacity to hold well-formed opinions to guide one's work and life.

**Social support:** To support the Sage, people need excellent school systems that foster an understanding of different learning styles and strategies for how to awaken latent curiosity and the desire to learn. Adults need access to lifelong learning, including retraining for new professions and careers when old ones become anachronistic. They also need press and media that provide information about critical issues, not just about who is using what strategy to win.

**In nature:** Intelligence and wisdom is housed in DNA (deoxyribonucleic acid, the molecular building blocks of life). The human body is "wise" in the ways of healing from the enzyme production that helps digest food to the antibodies that flood our bodies to fight infections. We know for example how easily most small cuts are healed without any action on our part: the body just knows what to do. In the environment around us, the Sage archetype can be exemplified in the Earth itself, which according to J. E. Lovelock's Gaia hypothesis, is a living organism, capable of shifting in response to new conditions (*Gaia: A New Look at Life on Earth*).

**In spirituality:** A major part of spiritual development comprises studying—reading, practice, listening to wise teachers—in an effort to understand and connect with the foundations of any spiritual practice. The Sage archetype helps many people utilize spiritual practices, such as prayer and meditation, as ways to connect with deep and reliable inner guidance. People often say that this wisdom comes from actual experience of the divine, not just what they have read from an authority.

**As leaders:** Sage leaders are excellent at dispassionate analysis, planning, evaluation, research, and making well-reasoned decisions. When others are panicking, they can detach, see the big picture, or take the long view and know what to do. They have a calming influence, and under such leadership events move forward at a measured pace, so that people can see that the right thing is being done in the right way.

If the Sage is active in your life, you
assume that "the truth will set you free."

**At your best** (now or when you fulfill your potential), you are not only knowledgeable but wise. You are wonderfully curious and love to think things through, striving as much as possible to filter out your own biases, to be as objective and fair as possible. You are motivated by a genuine hunger for truth and take a long-range perspective that prevents you from getting bogged down in petty squabbles and problems. You also see patterns in apparently discrepant events; you spot the error of logic or reasoning and practice paradigm vigilance, knowing how easy it is to be trapped by habits of mind or accepted ways of thinking things through. You excel at evaluating the merits of relative truths and commit to people and ideas even in the face of the realization that it is impossible to know anything for sure. You also have a gift for staying calm and unruffled.

**When problems emerge,** you typically research how others have addressed them before. Then you seek out the best process possible for thinking the issue through, finding an answer, and taking action to solve the problem. Finally you try to track and evaluate the results.

**You tend to notice** methodological flaws and to be rather slow to respond to situations unless they are urgent, because you see clearly how dangerous it is when people take action before they know what they are doing. By nature, you love ideas and the process of thinking, so you gravitate more toward the life of the mind than toward doing or experiencing. As a consequence, you may filter out "gut" or kinesthetic wisdom and facts that are not intellectually interesting.

**You may want to guard against** the Sage's tendency to be dogmatic and opinionated, with an ivory tower disdain for ordinary life and affairs. The keen ability of Sages to see the flaws in opinions and practices can take a negative or cynical turn, as they sit on the outside criticizing the efforts of others. Those expressing the Sage archetype may retreat to their heads, so they fail to act on what they know. Their emotions may take them over so that they act in snobbish or petty ways, masked by high-sounding principles and rhetoric.

**You like to be seen as** intelligent and perceptive, so you avoid revealing any areas of ignorance.

**Others may appreciate** your intelligence and expertise, or they can see you as nit-picky, living in an ivory tower, and irrelevant. They may seek you out as an advisor or enjoy trying to catch you in a mistake.

### Actions or qualities that you may find beneficial:

- Avoiding dogmatism and staying open to new information, even if it contradicts what you have thought previously.

- Paying attention to what works in the real world, rather than what simply delights the mind by its complexity.

- Communicating simply rather than showing off your genius.

- Staying in touch with gut or body knowledge.

- Balancing the virtues of the Sage with those of the Jester.

**If the Sage is one of your lowest scores,** you may do one or more of the following (check any that apply):

○ Lack studiousness or curiosity about things.

○ Not think things through very carefully, so you get yourself in unfortunate situations.

○ Think of intellectuals as nerdy and not very interesting or worthwhile.

○ Have the idea that you are not really very intelligent.

○ Have never had to actually think very deeply or study very much.

○ Have been told that you were not smart or that people who study are not doing anything valuable or real.

# NOTES

**JESTER**

*King Casimir of Poland loved merriment so much that he had two court Jesters. And when he learned that Tyll, the traveling Jester, was in the land, he invited him to the palace, too. Often the king's Jesters would argue, but when Tyll visited he would usually have the last word with his quick wit.*

*The king was determined to learn who was the cleverest Jester, so he devised a contest that was attended by the whole kingdom. After feasting and dancing, the king announced that he would offer twenty gold pieces to the Jester who could make the greatest wish.*

*The first Jester wished that the heavens be turned to paper and the sea to ink so he could have room to write the number that represented how much money he wished for. The second Jester wished for as many towers as there are stars so he would have space to store all the money wished by the first.*

*After a period of silence, Tyll spoke. "I wish," he mused, "that these two would name me in their wills to receive all their riches right before your majesty sends them to the gallows." The court filled with delighted laughter as Tyll left with the twenty gold pieces.*

Adapted from "Tyll Ulenspiegel's Merry Prank" in *Favorite Folktales from Around the World,* edited by Jane Yolen.

**The archetypal character:** The Jester character includes comics, clowns, humorists, and satirists as well as fun-loving people who bring laughter and enjoyment wherever they go. For the Jester, the purpose of life is to experience it fully, and those who express the Jester archetype try to find ways to enjoy unpleasant tasks or trick others into doing them (such as when Tom Sawyer gets his friends to pay him for the chance to paint a fence). The Jester within holds the secret to enjoying life.

**The archetypal plot:** The generic Jester plot is comic or edifying. Generally either the central character does very stupid things or the narrator makes fun of the stupid things others do, especially people in power.

Jester stories include slapstick comedies like Laurel and Hardy or the Marx Brothers. Such comedies revolve around the silly things people do, such as making slipping on a banana peel funny instead of dangerous. At the root of such comedies is the trickster, a popular figure in stories from many cultures, particularly Native American. The American Indian coyote was driven by his id (base desires such as hunger and lust) to get into all sorts of funny scrapes. These situations strike us as funny because they expose the parts of life we want to hide in our desire to seem sophisticated, virtuous, or important, and they provide some relief by reminding us of the humorous side of our undeveloped natures.

**Other stories that primarily concern the Jester:**

- Comic stories about painful events that help people accept difficulty, such as when people transform painful events into humorous anecdotes to tell their friends.

- Absurd narratives, such as the novels of Kurt Vonnegut, that describe difficult events humorously.

- Satire that reveals dishonesty through exaggeration, such as Jonathan Swift's essay from 1729, "A Modest Proposal," in which he suggests that the Irish eat their own children. This was his satirical effort to show how logic was being used to mask a lack of concern for others.

- Skits on late night talk shows or monologues and endless stories circulating through the Internet that ridicule the events of the day.

- Narratives about telling truth to power figures in a comic way. This can be the classic court Jester who acts as a foil to those in power, using wit to puncture pomposity and telling truths that others dare not say (as late night comics still do today).

- In a less friendly form, the Jester archetype can use satire to ridicule or put down another. This form of humor is often quite aggressive, a tool to win at another's expense or to undermine the authority of tyrants or incompetents in the family, the office, or anywhere else. (Examples are the *Emperor's New Clothes* or the TV series *The Office.*)

○ Stories about great times people have had, generally told with great energy and joy, even if those stories include escapades that might be really zany, dangerous, or even illegal. (Example: A good friend will bail you out of jail, but a great friend will sit with you on the bench, saying, "Damn that was fun.") Often these stories move us out of overly serious or moralistic ways of thinking.

○ Kindly humor as depicted in the film *The Search for Signs of Intelligent Life in the Universe* or Garrison Keillor's *News from Lake Wobegon*. Stories in which people are able to laugh at their own foibles as well as those of other people.

○ Spiritual narrative such as the teachings of the Sufi Nasrudin, which teach mystic truths through humor. In one such narrative that humorously demonstrates how we often cannot see what is right before us, Nasrudin tells of a border guard who witnessed Nasrudin coming through the checkpoint day after day with a wheelbarrow. The guard became convinced that Nasrudin was smuggling something but could not figure out what. (The punch line is that Nasrudin was smuggling wheelbarrows.)

**Imagery:** The classic Jester wore a three-point cap and bells, bright colors, and often ridiculous-looking bright-colored clothing with geometric designs. Today the Jester archetype is exemplified by silly stunts (people piling out of a very small car but acting as if what they are doing is normal). Those who express the Jester spirit might wear loud ties or scarves or bow ties with suspenders, signaling that they do not take themselves too seriously.

**Gifts:** The Jester knows better than any other archetype how to live in the present, savoring the pleasure of the moment. The Jester is also adept at knowing how to use humor to defuse anger, embarrassment, or conflict.

**Social support:** The Jester archetype is expressed in communities and social situations in many ways, including the passing on of jokes through the Internet, comedy shows, the entertainment industry, and a growing awareness in schools and businesses that playfulness increases creativity.

**In nature:** All mammals play, especially when they are young. Based on all the odd-looking creatures in the world, some consider Mother Nature to have a great sense of humor. The human ability to laugh is considered a survival advantage, one that to some degree helps people deal with real difficulties. Through human eyes, nature provides much that brings delight to our lives.

**In spirituality:** The holy fool, blissed out by the joy of divine presence, demonstrates the attainment of a level of joy that can only come from moving beyond the consciousness of the ego and beyond identification with the thoughts and worries of the mind. The ability to live wholly in the now is a mindful discipline of spiritual presence. Typically, the spiritual attainment of the Jester is free of concern for dogma or rules of behavior. However, the attainment of spiritual ecstasy may have been preceded by years of disciplined ascetic practices designed to foster an achievement of joy based on the genuine experience of divine rather than any prescriptions about belief or behavior.

**As leaders:** Leaders who embody the Jester archetype know how to make anything fun. They excel at divergent thinking in the way a joke makes us laugh because of the shift that requires us to see a surprising (and therefore often funny) perspective. Jester leaders are also good at being light-hearted about the challenges of organizational life. They encourage others to laugh rather than despair, and they can often come up with playful and creative ways of solving problems and realizing visions.

> If the Jester is active in your life, you
> assume that life is meant to be enjoyed.

**At your best** (now or when you fulfill your potential), you are happy, playful, funny, and fun to be around. In fact, you bring out the joy in life for everyone around you, showing others how to "be here now," to be playful and inventive, to enjoy the gift of living, even in stressful or difficult times. When everyone else is going crazy with fear and anxiety about how much change is going on in the world, instead of feeling anxious, you experience a rush of excitement. Instead of getting white-knuckled, you cry "Whee!" Like court Jesters and wise fools everywhere, you have a deep wisdom and use humor to say things with impunity that others might not want to hear. Implicitly politically *incorrect*, you are irreverent and apparently unconcerned with what others think. However, you know how to share what you think in ways that provoke laughter, not outrage. In fact, you find nothing more satisfying than making others laugh.

**You may want to guard against** the Jester's tendency to be irresponsible, to give in to overindulgence in pleasure seeking, or to play tricks or make cracks that may hurt people–or at the least hurt their feelings. You may also fail to take yourself seriously enough to fulfill your own dreams.

**When problems emerge,** you think outside the box. Having a trickster side, you know how to maneuver so that others help you out (Donkey in *Shrek*, talking his way out of difficulties). By nature, you also look for ways to enjoy the process of dealing with an issue–even if all you do is order pizzas so you (and others) can work through the night.

**Others may appreciate** your humor and enjoy being around you. They may also wish you would stop fooling around, settle down and be serious when its needed.

**You tend to notice** chances for fun in almost any situation, clever ways to get around obstacles, and the absurdities of life, which eventually become the basis of funny stories. Like a kid in a candy store, you are drawn to new experiences, the more the merrier. You may be a bit oblivious to the seriousness of situations or how seriously others are taking them.

**You want to be seen as** a fun person, so you try not to do or say anything that makes you seem boring or a drag on others. As a result, especially if you do not seem to be taking the situation seriously yourself, your clowning may make it difficult for others to help you when you need it.

**Actions or qualities that you may find beneficial:**

- Being certain to fulfill your responsibilities, even if they are boring.
- Finding fun ways to do work that might seem routine or dull.
- Remembering to have empathy for how others may experience your jokes.
- Taking time to clarify your values and protect what and who are really precious to you.
- Practicing moderation and common sense.
- Balancing the virtues of the Jester with those of the Sage.

**If the Jester is one of your lowest scores,** you may do one or more of the following (check any that apply):

○ Have a hard time lightening up and just having fun.

○ Be seen by others as overly serious or boring or as someone who cannot take a joke.

○ Find people who are always cutting up really annoying.

○ Experience life as difficult so you cannot think of much to enjoy or be happy about.

○ Have been taught that life is a serious matter and that people who have a lot of fun are shirking important responsibilities.

# NOTES

CHAPTER 9

# Resources for Expanding Your Skills

## Books

*PMAI® Manual: A Guide to Interpreting the Pearson-Marr Archetype Indicator® Instrument* by Carol S. Pearson and Hugh K. Marr (2003 CAPT)

> This official manual for the PMAI® instrument helps individuals and professionals study the background, theories, and psychometrics of the PMAI® archetype instrument. Included are case studies, reliability and validity studies, and suggested uses.

*Awakening the Heroes Within: Twelve Archetypes to Help Us Find Ourselves and Transform Our World* by Carol S. Pearson (1991 HarperSanFrancisco)

> The PMAI® instrument was based on the model developed in this book, which provides an in-depth understanding of the twelve archetypes. A number of learning exercises are included.

*Depth Coaching: Discovering Archetypes for Empowerment, Growth, and Balance* by Patricia R. Adson (2004 CAPT)

> This book is ideal for psychotherapists and counselors to use first for their own journeys and then with clients; and for individuals to use for personal growth or

for helping others on the journey to self-development. Based on the work of Carol S. Pearson, *Depth Coaching* walks the reader through the hero's journey, providing details about the ego, soul, and self and about the three stages of the journey. Each section is followed by a workbook.

*The Hero Within: Six Archetypes We Live By* by Carol S. Pearson (1998 HarperSanFrancisco)

This best-selling book on archetypes and the heroic journey discusses six archetypes relevant to success in today's world. It is easy to read and includes an in-depth analysis of how to work with archetypes in your life.

*Mapping the Organizational Psyche: A Jungian Theory of Organizational Dynamics and Change* by John G. Corlett and Carol S. Pearson (2003 CAPT)

This book provides an exciting and innovative way to look at and better understand organizations. Basing their work on that of C.G. Jung, the authors present both theoretical and practical approaches for stakeholders to explore the organizational unconscious. Practical solutions are presented through the concepts of archetypes. What story is your company living? Is it the path that needs to be taken? A workbook section is included to allow readers to assess their own organizations.

*The Hero and the Outlaw: Building Extraordinary Brands through the Power of Archetypes* by Margaret Mark and Carol S. Pearson (McGraw-Hill 2002)

Learn about the importance of branding in today's corporate world and discover how brand names influence our lives. *The Hero and the Outlaw* offers clearly structured systems that businesses and marketing professionals can follow and replicate. Through this system, a company can connect more deeply with customers and derive the most from the expensive marketing campaigns that support today's brand names. This book is also of interest to general readers who want to understand advertising from an archetypal perspective.

## PMAI® Assessment Online

The Pearson-Marr Archetype Indicator® (PMAI®) assessment is available online at **www.capt.org** so that you can take the instrument from time to time to see how the archetypes expressed in your life may be changing. In addition, the online version makes it easy and cost effective for a friend, spouse, family, or group to take the instrument so that each person receives his or her personal results and a copy of an introductory book.

## Seminars and Classes

From time to time the publisher offers seminars about uses and applications for the PMAI®
instrument. For more information about these programs, visit the training section of the Center
for Applications of Psychological Type web site, www.capt.org

## Applications, Case Studies, and Research

The Pearson–Marr Archetype Indicator® instrument is a valuable tool for use in many areas
of personal and professional development, including counseling, team building, business and
life coaching, working with families and relationships, and seeking spiritual paths. The authors
and the publisher have an ongoing interest in applications and case studies regarding use of
the PMAI® instrument. If you have examples of how you have used the instrument or if you
have a research project in mind, please contact the CAPT Research Department at research@
capt.org

## Contact Information

### Center for Applications of Psychological Type (CAPT)

2815 NW 13th Street, Suite 401

Gainesville, FL 32609 USA

800.777.2278 (*toll-free USA and Canada only*)

352.375.0160

www.capt.org

### Center for Archetypal Studies and Applications (CASA)

www.herowithin.com

# NOTES

# References

Andersen, H. C. 1999. *The Little Match Girl.* Trans. and illus. by J. Pinckney. New York: Puffin Books.

Campbell, J. 1990. *Transformation of Myth Through Time.* New York: Harper & Row.

--------- 1973. *Campbell's Myths to Live By.* New York: Bantam Books.

Coelho, P. 1998. *The Alchemist.* New York: HarperSanFrancisco.

Goetz, D. and S. G. Morley. 1954. *Popol Vuh: The Book of the People.* Trans. Adrian Recino. (See also "Pre-Columbian Antecedents for Modern Highland Mayan Ceremonialism" at www.hummet.ucla.edu/humnet/arthist/icono/christenson/maya.htm.)

Goleman, D. 1997. *Emotional Intelligence: Why It Can Matter More than IQ.* New York: Bantam Books.

Hamilton, E. 1969. *Mythology: Timeless Tales of Gods and Heroes.* New York: New American Library.

Kegan, R. 1994. *In Over Our Heads: The Mental Demands of Modern Life.* Cambridge, MA: Harvard University Press.

Littleton, C. S., ed. 2002. "Mother of the World" in *Mythology: The Illustrated Anthology of World Myth and Storytelling.* London: Duncan Baird.

--------- "Demeter's Tale of Death and Rebirth" in *Mythology: The Illustrated Anthology of World Myth and Storytelling.* London: Duncan Baird.

--------- "Spirit of the Ancestral Sisters" in *Mythology: The Illustrated Anthology of World Myth and Storytelling.* London: Duncan Baird.

--------- "The Time of Ten Suns" in *Mythology: The Illustrated Anthology of World Myth and Storytelling.* London: Duncan Baird.

Lönnrot, E. 1888/1999. *The Kalevala.* New York: Oxford University Press.

Merriam-Webster, 2002. *Webster's Third New International Dictionary, Unabridged.* http://unabridged.merriam-webster.com (June 19, 2006).

Staines, D. 1993. *The Complete Romances of Chrétien de Troyes.* Bloomington, IN: Indiana University Press.

Steptoe, J. 1972. *The Story of Jumping Mouse.* New York: HarperTrophy.

Storm, H. 1972. *Seven Arrows.* New York: Ballantine Books.

Van Dyke, H. 1899. *The Story of the Other Wise Man.* New York: Harper & Brothers.

Whedbee, C. H. 1966. "The Witch of Nag's Head Woods" in *Legends of the Outer Banks and Tar Heel Tidewater.* Winston-Salem, N.C.: John F. Blair.

Yolen, J., ed. 1986. "Tyll Ulenspiegel's Merry Prank" from *Favorite Folktales from Around the World.* New York: Pantheon Books.

--------- "It Could Always Be Worse" from *Favorite Folktales from Around the World.* New York: Pantheon Books.

# NOTES

# AUTHORS

**Carol S. Pearson, Ph.D.,** is Executive Vice President and Provost of Pacifica Graduate Institute located in Carpinteria, California. Prior to this appointment, she was the director of the James MacGregor Burns Academy of Leadership and a Professor of Leadership Studies in the School of Public Policy at the University of Maryland.

Her work utilizes concepts from Jungian psychology that deepen and enrich the experience in people's lives that encourage the narrative intelligence required to make choices that are healthy, productive, and full of possibilities. Her publications related to these interests include *The Hero Within: Six Archetypes We Live By; Awakening the Heroes Within: Twelve Archetypes that Help Us Find Ourselves and Transform Our World; The Hero and the Outlaw: Building Extraordinary Brands Through the Power of Archetypes,* coauthored by Margaret Mark; and *Mapping the Organizational Psyche: A Jungian Theory of Organizational Dynamics and Change,* coauthored by John Corlett. Several of her books are available in a growing number of foreign languages.

Dr. Pearson, along with Dr. Hugh Marr, created the Pearson-Marr Archetype Indicator® (PMAI®) assessment. She teaches and speaks about archetypes, narrative intelligence, as well as consults in the areas of leadership development, organizational culture, and integrated branding.

**Hugh K. Marr, Ph.D.,** is both a licensed clinical psychologist and a licensed professional counselor in the private practice of psychotherapy in Alexandria, Virginia. He specializes in working with trauma and its impact on both substance abuse and on couple relationships. Dr. Marr teaches trauma therapy as well as group and individual psychotherapy to graduate students at The American School of Professional Psychology/Argosy University, and consults to Intensive Trauma Therapy in Morgantown, West Virginia. He has more than 30 years of clinical experience, and is a long-time student of narrative and Jungian psychology. Dr. Marr's work on archetypes influences his clinical work and his teaching. Dr. Marr consults to mental health and substance abuse programs and is available for workshops, presentations, and clinical supervision.

# NOTES

# NOTES